ATLAS OF
SOCIAL ISSUES

ATLAS OF SOCIAL ISSUES

DR. ALISDAIR ROGERS

Lecturer in Social and Cultural Geography
Keble College and Lady Margaret Hall
Oxford University

Oxford University Press 1990

Published by

Oxford University Press, Walton Street, Oxford OX2 6DP
Oxford New York Toronto Delhi Bombay Calcutta Madras
Karachi Petaling Jaya Singapore Hong Kong Tokyo Nairobi
Dar es Salaam Cape Town Melbourne Auckland

and associated companies in Berlin and Ibadan
Oxford is a trademark of Oxford University Press

ISBN 0 19 913374 3

An Ilex book

Created and produced by Ilex Publishers Limited
29–31 George Street, Oxford OX1 2AJ

Designed by John Downes and Simon Taylor

Illustrated by Steve Weston and John Downes

Typesetting by Opus, Oxford
Colour separations by Columbia Offset, Scantrans Pte. Ltd.
Printed in Spain

Contents

1 Fertility control

At the World Population Conference in Mexico City in 1984 most of the world's governments recognized a need to take active steps to control fertility levels and slow down rates of population growth. Countries which had already introduced widespread family planning programmes, such as China, India, Mexico and Thailand, had achieved considerable success. These countries feared that rising population numbers would put pressure on land, food, resources, education, health and other services.

Their experience suggested that there was no one way to reduce fertility levels. It was neither enough to introduce contraceptive technology such as the pill and condom, nor to start programmes of sterilization. The social, economic and cultural background was also important. In particular the more control women had over their lives the more likely they were to want fewer children. In much of the world families depend upon children for both labour and supporting the old, and until alternative sources of assistance become available it makes good economic sense to have large families.

In some ways, therefore, development is the best form of contraception. But many governments feel that they cannot wait and hope for economic growth, and given the long time that elapses before any population policy takes effect, they feel they must act immediately.

Falling fertility

A common measure of fertility is the Total Fertility Rate (TFR), which is the number of children born to the average woman. In 1950 the world TFR was 5.0, and in 1987 3.6, but with great geographical variations (as the map shows). To maintain population size a TFR of 2.1 is required. This is know as the *replacement level*, and many industrialized countries have fallen below it. There are now fears of future labour shortages and a lack of working-age people to support the young and old.

China

The world's most drastic and successful programme to reduce fertility started in China in 1971. The government set a standard of two children per family, which was reduced to one in the 1980s. Couples having only one child gained higher pensions, better housing, and free health care, while those having more than two received penalties. The campaign has so far been generally successful, especially in urban areas. Many rural families feared that there would be no one to look after them in old age and did not comply.

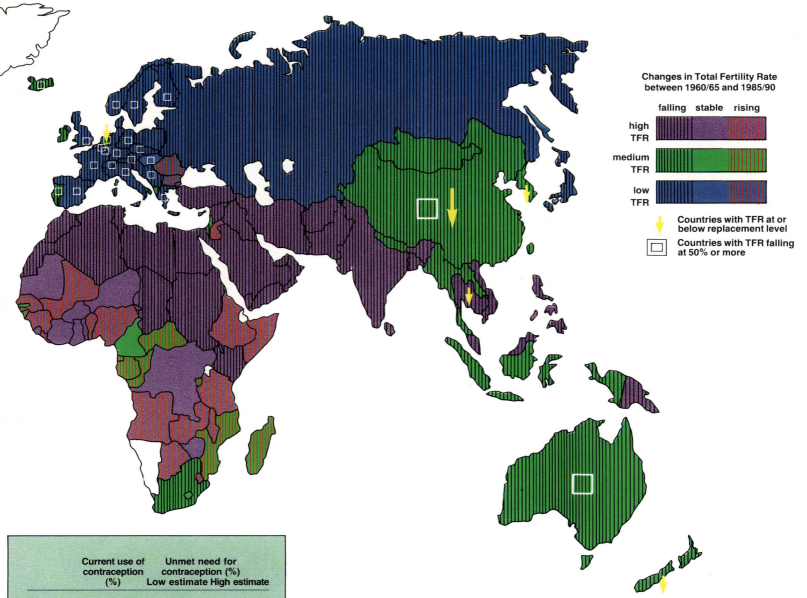

Changes in Total Fertility Rate between 1960/65 and 1985/90

	falling	stable	rising
high TFR			
medium TFR			
low TFR			

↓ Countries with TFR at or below replacement level

☐ Countries with TFR falling at 50% or more

	Current use of contraception (%)	Unmet need for contraception (%)	
		Low estimate	High estimate
Sudan	5	6	9
Pakistan	5	17	27
Kenya	7	6	10
Bangladesh	19	25	28
Honduras	27	9	21
Sri Lanka	55	18	31
Thailand	59	11	29

Use of contraception

The World Fertility Survey (1972–84) found that, in virtually all developing countries surveyed, the number of women of childbearing age who wanted no more children was greater than the number using some form of effective contraception. This unmet need varied from 1 to 30% of married women, suggesting that there is much scope for the wider distribution of, and education about, contraception. Actual use varied from less than 5% of women in Pakistan, Senegal and Sudan, to over 60% in the industrialized world.

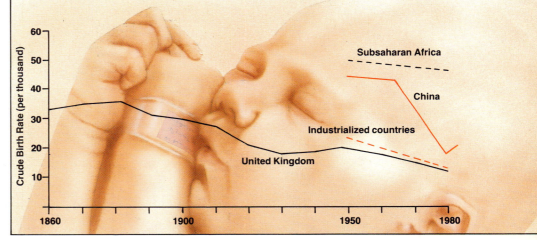

Decline in time

A combination of strong central government, economic growth and the availability of contraception has enabled some developing countries to reduce their crude birth rates (the number of live births per 1000 population) much more rapidly than developed countries did in the past. The shift from high to low levels took a century in the United Kingdom, but only 30 years in China.

2 The Young

In the post-war era the world's birth rate rose to record levels, and although fertility rates are now falling in most countries the world's population has gained a 'big bulge' of young children. One-third of the Earth's inhabitants are under 14 years old.

The health of a country's young is often the best indicator of its social and economic health. Children are the first to suffer in times of famine and economic stress. The countries with the youngest populations generally also have the highest rates of infant mortality. Although rates have fallen, and in some places been halved, the survival of children in developing countries has become one of the world's priorities. The United Nations Children's Fund is leading a campaign to save children's lives, mostly through simple and inexpensive means.

Other major priorities include education and child labour. Although the International Labour Organization has tried to fix a minimum age of employment at 15, there may be up to 50 million children working in exploitative conditions such as in mines and sweatshops. Of equal concern is the plight of thousands of children sold for prostitution throughout the world. This 20th-century slave trade takes children from the poorest countries to satisfy customers in the wealthier West. For these and other reasons the United Nations is considering a special Convention on the Rights of the Child to give to the young the protection already afforded to adults.

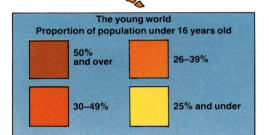

The young world
Proportion of population under 16 years old

■	50% and over	■	26–39%
■	30–49%	■	25% and under

N.A.

Proposed UN children's charter

The proposed Convention on the Rights of the Child will safeguard the welfare and special needs of children throughout the world. It covers such issues as survival rights (health care, food and shelter), protection from abuse and exploitation, and the right to education. It encourages governments to act in the best interests of children and to introduce laws to protect them.

Prostitution is a way of life for many children, not only in Latin America and South-East Asia but in large Western cities such as London and Amsterdam. In Paris alone there may be as many as 8000 children involved.

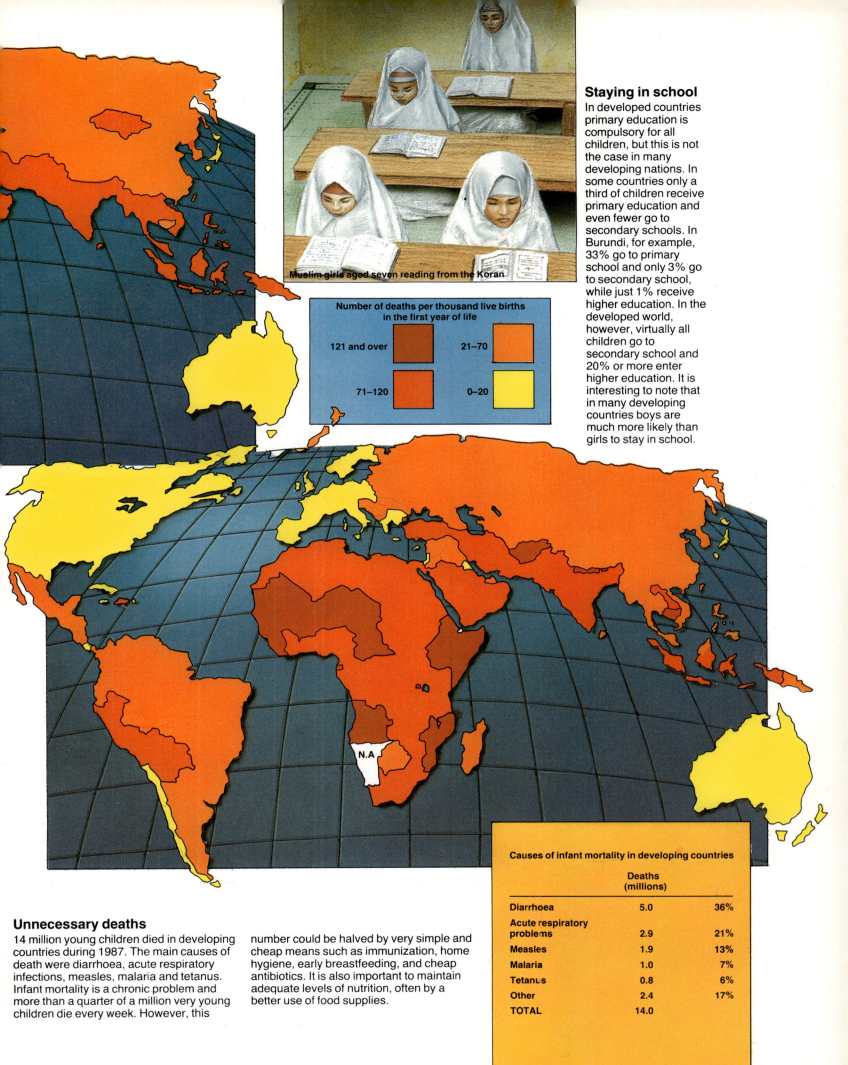

Staying in school

In developed countries primary education is compulsory for all children, but this is not the case in many developing nations. In some countries only a third of children receive primary education and even fewer go to secondary schools. In Burundi, for example, 33% go to primary school and only 3% go to secondary school, while just 1% receive higher education. In the developed world, however, virtually all children go to secondary school and 20% or more enter higher education. It is interesting to note that in many developing countries boys are much more likely than girls to stay in school.

Muslim girls aged seven reading from the Koran

Number of deaths per thousand live births in the first year of life

121 and over	21–70
71–120	0–20

N.A

Unnecessary deaths

14 million young children died in developing countries during 1987. The main causes of death were diarrhoea, acute respiratory infections, measles, malaria and tetanus. Infant mortality is a chronic problem and more than a quarter of a million very young children die every week. However, this number could be halved by very simple and cheap means such as immunization, home hygiene, early breastfeeding, and cheap antibiotics. It is also important to maintain adequate levels of nutrition, often by a better use of food supplies.

Causes of infant mortality in developing countries

	Deaths (millions)	
Diarrhoea	5.0	36%
Acute respiratory problems	2.9	21%
Measles	1.9	13%
Malaria	1.0	7%
Tetanus	0.8	6%
Other	2.4	17%
TOTAL	14.0	

9

3 The Old

In 1980 only 8.5% of the world's population was aged 60 years or over. But as global rates of fertility continue to fall, the United Nations forecasts that the proportion will rise to 14% by the year 2025. Global ageing is a recent event, following the youth explosion of the post-war decades. The trend was led by the developed countries but the rest of the world is catching up as today's young become tomorrow's elderly.

Age is a difficult concept. There is no clear definition of what is 'old', but in societies where a person's status and livelihood is commonly defined by work, retirement often marks a key turning point. In the West, although retirement is usually between the ages of 60 and 67, state pensions, private savings and better health are encouraging people to leave work earlier. In some African countries, by contrast, although government workers can retire at 55, most people must continue working to support themselves.

The old are often seen as a social problem in the West. They tend to be poorer, in worse health, and more likely to live alone than the rest of the population. There are fewer working-age people to pay the taxes to support the welfare and medical needs of a growing number of elderly. However some elderly people are finding new roles, often contributing their time, energy, and expertise to a wide range of voluntary causes. Today's elderly are literally living on a new and as yet only partly explored 'age frontier', and societies still need to discover how best to use this valuable human resource.

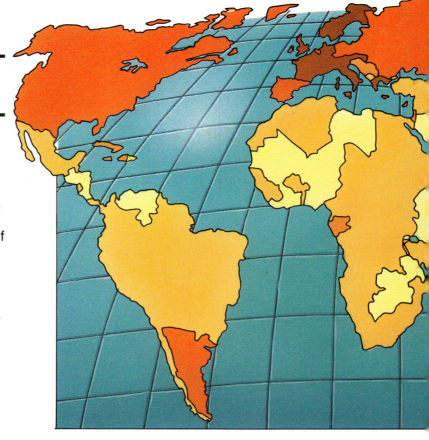

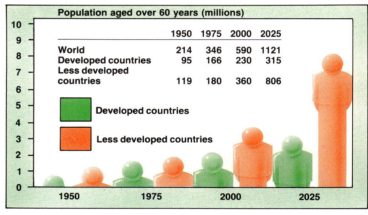

Population aged over 60 years (millions)

	1950	1975	2000	2025
World	214	346	590	1121
Developed countries	95	166	230	315
Less developed countries	119	180	360	806

Developed countries

Less developed countries

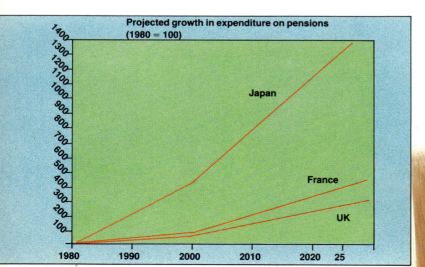

Projected growth in expenditure on pensions (1980 = 100)

Japan

France

UK

The economics of ageing

The largest item of social expenditure in the seven major developed countries is pensions. As the elderly population increases, such expenditures will rise. Demographers use an indicator called 'the elderly dependency rate', which is the ratio of the population aged 65 and over to the potential working-age population (aged 15–64).

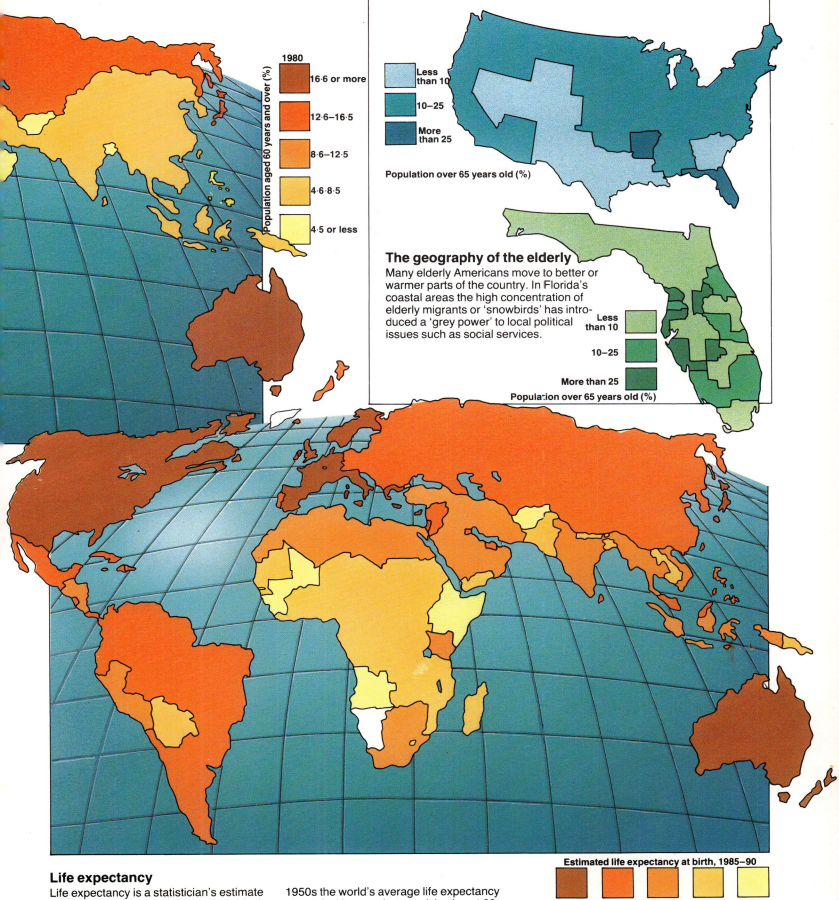

The geography of the elderly

Many elderly Americans move to better or warmer parts of the country. In Florida's coastal areas the high concentration of elderly migrants or 'snowbirds' has introduced a 'grey power' to local political issues such as social services.

Life expectancy

Life expectancy is a statistician's estimate of the number of years a typical individual born in a given period can expect to live. Since it is an average for the whole population it does not mean, of course, that, for example, a Bolivian will die when he or she reaches 57 years of age. In fact, low life expectancies are generally the result of high rates of infant mortality. In the 1950s the world's average life expectancy was only 46 years, but now it is almost 60. There are considerable variations between countries, from 36 years in Sierra Leone to 77 years in Iceland. Generally, women live two to five years longer than men, except in a few South Asian countries where their low social status can lead to shorter lifespans.

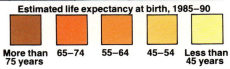

4 Urban Explosion

Between 1980 and 2000 there will be a further 1 billion people inhabiting the cities of the developing world. The urban populations of Africa and South Asia will more than double.

The problems posed by rapid urbanization stem not only from high population growth rates. In the West, the urban explosion resulted from industry's massive demand for labour, which was initially provided by rural migrants. But in developing countries innovations in technology and industry have meant that industrial growth no longer depends upon such a large number of workers. Thus, while agricultural areas become modernized and mechanized, urban industry cannot absorb the surplus rural workforce.

Many countries are therefore starting to encourage rural and agricultural projects. China actively restricts rural migration but also locates small-scale industry and health services in rural areas. Brazil has tried to open up the resources of the Amazon region, while Mali and Somalia have attempted to concentrate dispersed rural populations in a smaller number of large villages. The success of such schemes depends, to a large extent, on stable prices of agricultural commodities on the world market.

Urban
Rican

Rural-urban migration

Brazil is typical of a developing country undergoing rapid urbanization and rural depopulation, with high rates of rural-urban migration. By contrast, Kenya shows that both urban and rural populations may increase at the same time, due to high birth rates. It is not predicted to become a predominantly urban country until well into the next century. France represents a situation in which decades of rural decline and urban growth are being followed by a period of stability, in which the rural population is maintained.

A desert shanty town surrounds Nouakchott, capital city of Mauritania.

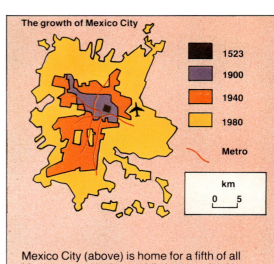

The growth of Mexico City

Mexico City (above) is home for a fifth of all Mexicans and is the world's largest city. It covers twice the area of New York City and is growing fast. Unlike most Third World cities, however, it is rural-urban migration rather than a high birth rate which explains its rapid growth.

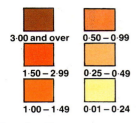

3·00 and over	0·50 – 0·99
1·50 – 2·99	0·25 – 0·49
1·00 – 1·49	0·01 – 0·24

Urbanization

The two maps show the ratio of urban to rural populations for 1950 and 2000 (projected). A ratio of one means that the urban and rural populations are equal in size; below one means that the rural population is larger; above one means that the urban population is larger.

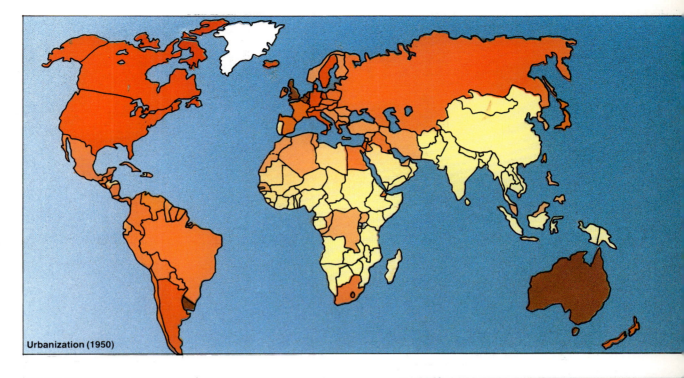

Urbanization (1950)

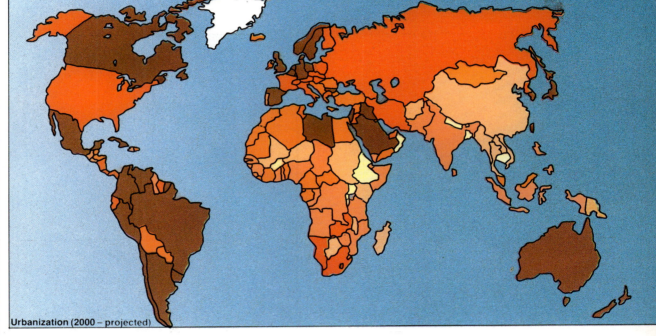

Urbanization (2000 – projected)

Better off in the city?

It is often thought by outsiders that rural migrants go to cities with unrealistic expectations that life will be better there. In fact, urban wages, employment, health services, schools, and basic services such as water and sanitation are generally above the level of rural areas, which may also be more overcrowded. Moving to a city gives the migrant and his children a chance of a better life, which may not even be a possibility in rural areas.

Percentage of population with adequate access to:

	Water	
	Urban	Rural
Kenya	97	15
Mexico	64	43
Bolivia	69	10
India	77	31
Indonesia	35	19

	Sanitation	
	Urban	Rural
Kenya	89	19
Mexico	51	12
Bolivia	37	4
India	27	1
Indonesia	29	21

City dwellers of the future

Twenty years ago the majority of the world's millionaire cities were in the developed world. Today, because of increased commuting in the West, (which stabilizes the growth of major cities by allowing people to live in areas which may be quite long distances away from where they work), and rapid urbanization in developing countries, it is thought that by the year 2000 85% of all new urban dwellers will be in the developing countries: two-thirds of all millionaire cities and three-quarters of all 4-million cities will be in the developing world. This urban explosion is led by Latin America, but Africa and Asia are now also entering phases of rapid urbanization.

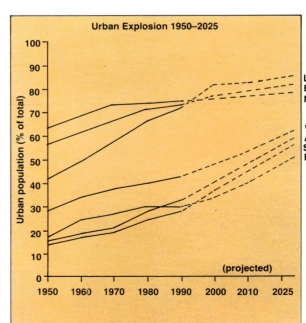

Urban Explosion 1950–2025

5 Megalopolis

The term 'megalopolis' is used to define areas where once distinct cities have grown so large that their suburbs have merged with those of neighbouring cities. The countryside between them has been swallowed up by urban development and huge urban agglomerations are the result. These have often developed in the great manufacturing centres of the world. The first region to be described as a megalopolis was an area of the United States eastern seaboard, stretching from Boston to Washington. Other 'supercities' with populations of over 10 million people are found in the Rhine-Ruhr region of West Germany, North-Eastern China, the Great Lakes of North America and Southern California.

Although large cities have problems, they are not necessarily unmanageable. Large cities often benefit from economies of scale. It is cheaper to provide services such as roads and hospitals for large concentrations of people, and employers gain from the increased numbers of skilled workers. For developing countries it is often economically efficient to concentrate scarce resources on a single place. However, for some rapidly growing cities the problems are insurmountable. Some cities in the developing world gain 140,000 new residents every day and the provision of basic services cannot keep up with demand.

The big ten cities (populations given in millions)

1 Mexico City (25·8)
2 São Paulo (24·0)
3 Tokyo/ Yokohama (20·2)
4 Calcutta (16·5)
5 Greater Bombay (16·0)
6 New York/New Jersey (15·8)
7 Seoul (13·8)
8 Tehran (13·6)
9 Shanghai (13·3)
10 Rio de Janeiro (13·3)

Big numbers, high costs

The concentration of people and investment in large cities can have negative consequences, pushing up the cost of land, housing and wages. In central Tokyo, a piece of land the size of this book could cost £10,000. More people also means more traffic. The number of vehicles entering London during peak hours has increased 22% in the past decade, while average speeds have dropped to 13 kph in the centre, hardly faster than a horse-drawn carriage. Ideally, high prices and congestion should encourage people and companies to move elsewhere, but this usually happens far too slowly, if at all. Urban planning often tries to force decentralization, through new towns.

Traffic congestion is now a common experience in all the world's major cities. In many cities of the developed world average traffic speeds are now falling to levels much the same as the horse-drawn transport of a hundred years ago. Such delays cost money in terms of lost time, wasted fuel, and pollution. In the past the answer was to build more roads or rail systems. Today increasingly tough measures are being introduced. These include complete bans in some town centres and charging directly for road use.

City of freeways and smog

In the mid-19th century Los Angeles had a population of only 8,000. Today it is the centre of an urban region of over 12 million inhabitants. This rapid growth took place in the era of the automobile, making Los Angeles uniquely dependent on cars and freeways. The result has been intense smog and traffic congestion. City planners hope, however, that the new subway system will help counter these effects.

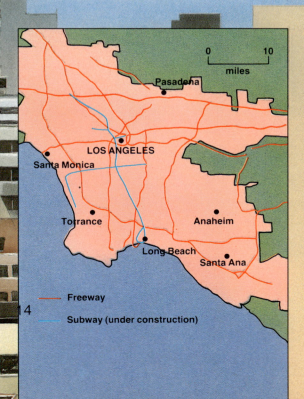

0   10
miles

— Freeway
— Subway (under construction)

14

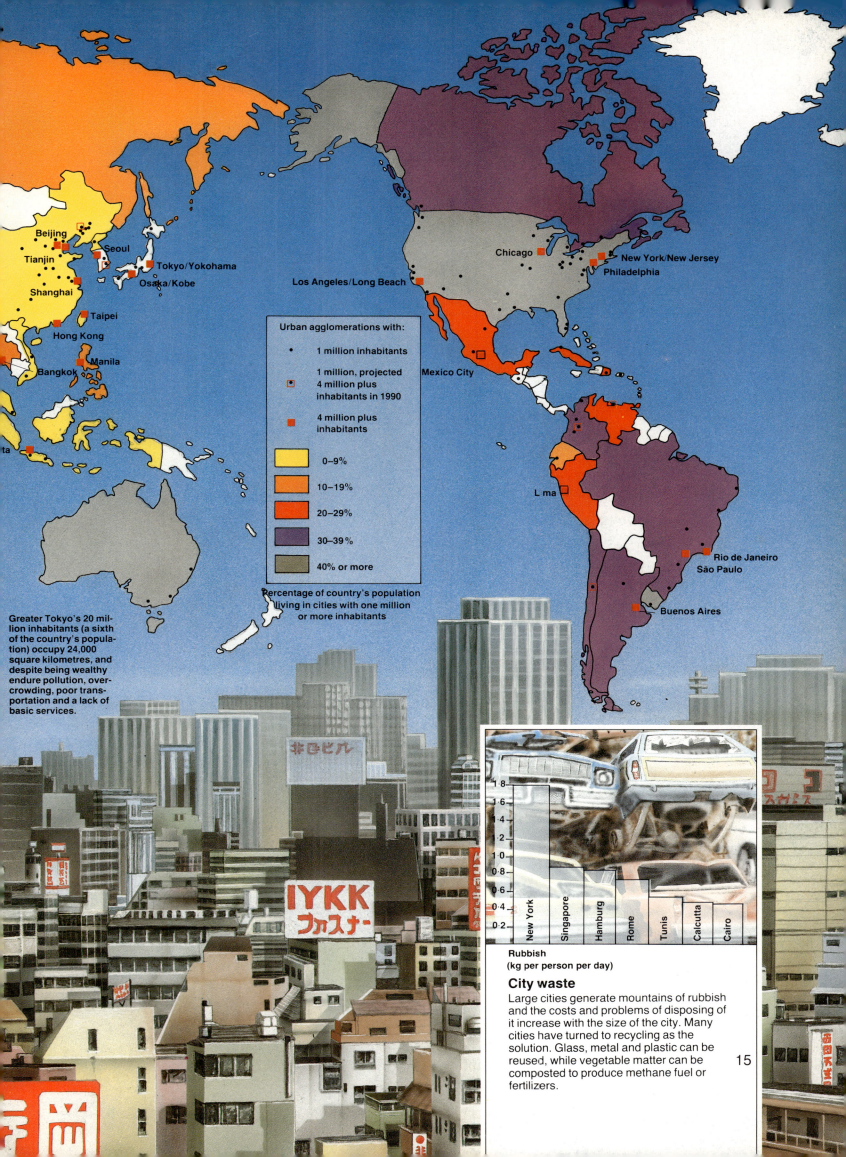

Urban agglomerations with:

· 1 million inhabitants

◉ 1 million, projected 4 million plus inhabitants in 1990

◼ 4 million plus inhabitants

Percentage of country's population living in cities with one million or more inhabitants

	0–9%
	10–19%
	20–29%
	30–39%
	40% or more

Beijing
Tianjin
Seoul
Tokyo/Yokohama
Osaka/Kobe
Shanghai
Taipei
Hong Kong
Manila
Bangkok

Chicago
New York/New Jersey
Philadelphia
Los Angeles/Long Beach
Mexico City
Lima
Rio de Janeiro
São Paulo
Buenos Aires

Greater Tokyo's 20 million inhabitants (a sixth of the country's population) occupy 24,000 square kilometres, and despite being wealthy endure pollution, overcrowding, poor transportation and a lack of basic services.

Rubbish
(kg per person per day)

New York
Singapore
Hamburg
Rome
Tunis
Calcutta
Cairo

City waste

Large cities generate mountains of rubbish and the costs and problems of disposing of it increase with the size of the city. Many cities have turned to recycling as the solution. Glass, metal and plastic can be reused, while vegetable matter can be composted to produce methane fuel or fertilizers.

15

6 Rural change

Fundamental changes are occurring in the world's rural areas. In the largely agricultural economies of the developing world, land reform, mineral extraction, rural migration and agricultural change combine to alter lifestyles and cultures. New trends have also emerged in the industrialized world. Alongside regions of rural population and economic decline, are regions of 'counter-urbanization'.

Counter-urbanization is the reversal of the historic pattern of urban population growth and rural population decrease. It is associated with the emergence of economic activity not tied to urban areas or natural resources, such as high-technology manufacturing, tourism, and other service industries. While the movement of some people into the countryside is the result of spillover from large urban centres and consists largely of commuters, a growing proportion seems to consist of people who both live and work in the countryside and its small towns. Such 'counter-urbanization' has been observed in the US and throughout much of Europe, where it is also referred to as a 'rural renaissance' and an 'urban turnaround'.

Although this process may help rural economies, it can also lead to rising house prices, the blocking of further development and conservation.

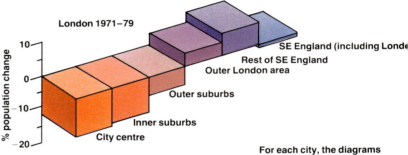

Paris 1968–75

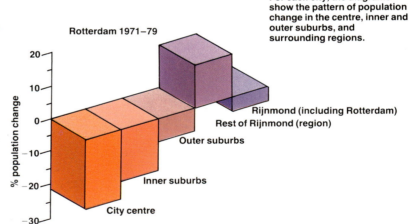

London 1971–79

Rotterdam 1971–79

For each city, the diagrams show the pattern of population change in the centre, inner and outer suburbs, and surrounding regions.

Resistance to change

In Europe's 'Celtic fringe', which includes Ireland, Scotland, Wales, Cornwall and Brittany, counter-urbanization has coincided with a cultural revival based upon local languages. In some circumstances the potential conflict between wealthy newcomers and the existing rural community becomes open hostility. Many Welsh speakers are concerned that their children may no longer be taught Welsh in schools dominated by outsiders. The purchase of second homes has also caused strife and some holiday cottages have been burned in Wales.

Brittany

From the mid-19th to mid-20th centuries Brittany experienced high levels of out-migration which, at times, were hardly balanced by natural increase. But between 1968 and 1975 migrants started moving in, reversing the decline. As the table shows, it is now the smaller, more remote settlements which are growing fastest. This revival depends heavily on tourism, and Brittany receives three million visitors a year.

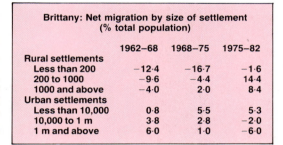

Brittany: Net migration by size of settlement (% total population)			
	1962–68	1968–75	1975–82
Rural settlements			
Less than 200	−12·4	−16·7	−1·6
200 to 1000	−9·6	−4·4	14·4
1000 and above	−4·0	2·0	8·4
Urban settlements			
Less than 10,000	0·8	5·5	5·3
10,000 to 1 m	3·8	2·8	−2·0
1 m and above	6·0	1·0	−6·0

Pockets of poverty

Although poverty is commonly thought of as being a phenomenon of inner cities, in some ways rural poverty is a more serious condition. In the USA, 14.5% of rural families are below the official poverty line, compared with 11.1% of urban families. The rural poor suffer problems of access to jobs and services and pay higher prices for goods in small rural shops. Pockets of persistent rural poverty are associated with underfunded small farms in areas where there are few alternative jobs. When young able-bodied workers migrate from such areas they leave behind an older, more dependent population.

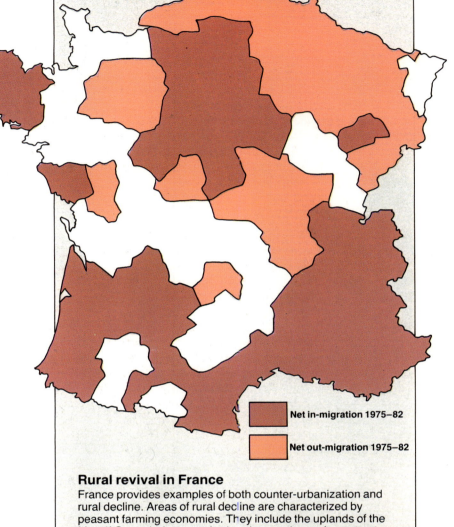

Net in-migration 1975–82

Net out-migration 1975–82

Rural revival in France

France provides examples of both counter-urbanization and rural decline. Areas of rural decline are characterized by peasant farming economies. They include the uplands of the Massif Central where rural migration continues. In contrast, the outer Paris region, the southeast or Midi, and the Atlantic coast have enjoyed an economic boom based on a combination of tourism, light industry (including high-technology firms) and modernized agriculture.

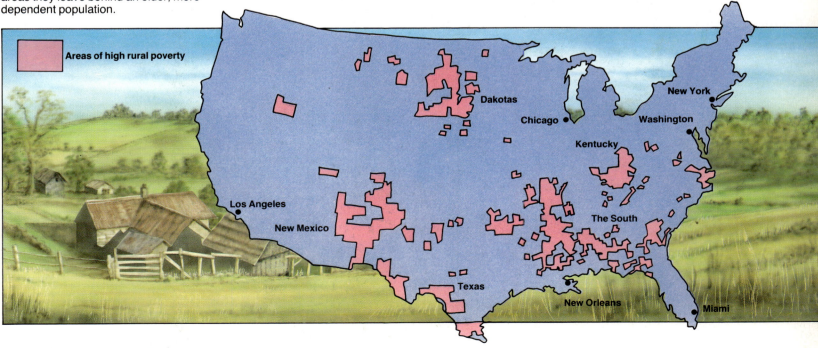

Areas of high rural poverty

Dakotas
New York
Chicago
Washington
Kentucky
Los Angeles
New Mexico
The South
Texas
New Orleans
Miami

7 Rich and Poor

The poorest half of the world's population receives only 5% of its income, while the richest 5% controls two-thirds of the wealth. This wealth gap is also evident within countries. It is generally true to say that during the early stages of development inequality between rich and poor increases, but declines later, although many argue that the 1980s have seen the gap between rich and poor widening again even in relatively prosperous countries.

Governments trying to create a more equal distribution of wealth have four main options. *Taxation on earnings* tends to have only minor effects, is easy to avoid, and can be a disincentive to work. *Direct cash payments* to the poor by the state has worked well in the West, but as a policy it is costly to administer. *Subsidies* to health, housing, and education are also beneficial. Finally, governments may *redistribute assets* such as land. Socialist countries dedicated to the principles of equality and redistribution by curbing private ownership of property and wealth have gone the furthest in closing the gap, although socialist economies have great difficulties in increasing overall prosperity.

Safety nets

The map shows which countries have unemployment benefit and/or family allowance, i.e., money paid to families to help them bring up children. Such payments provide a safety net for those who would otherwise be plunged into poverty. The effect of such laws varies considerably; not all persons may be eligible, and the period for which the benefit is paid also changes from country to country. Many socialist countries have no such benefit, since they guarantee every worker a job and do not officially recognize unemployment.

Share of National Income held by:

- Top fifth of households (blue)
- Fourth fifth (pink)
- Third fifth (green)
- Second fifth (yellow)
- Bottom fifth (white)

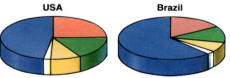

USA   Brazil

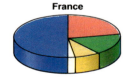

France

UK

East Germany

Wealth gap

These maps show the unequal distribution of income among households in a given country. The gap is calculated by taking the difference between the shares of wealth held by the richest and poorest fifths of all households. So, for example, in Brazil (the most unequal country), the richest 20% of all households have 66·6% of total income, while the poorest 20% have only 2% of all income. The difference, or wealth gap, is 64·6%, a high figure.

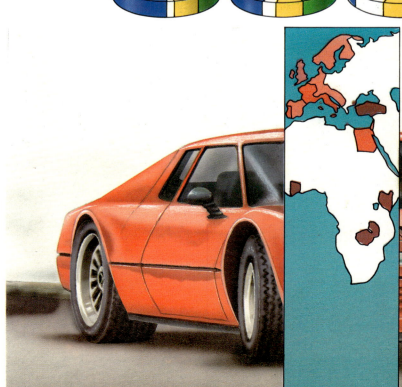

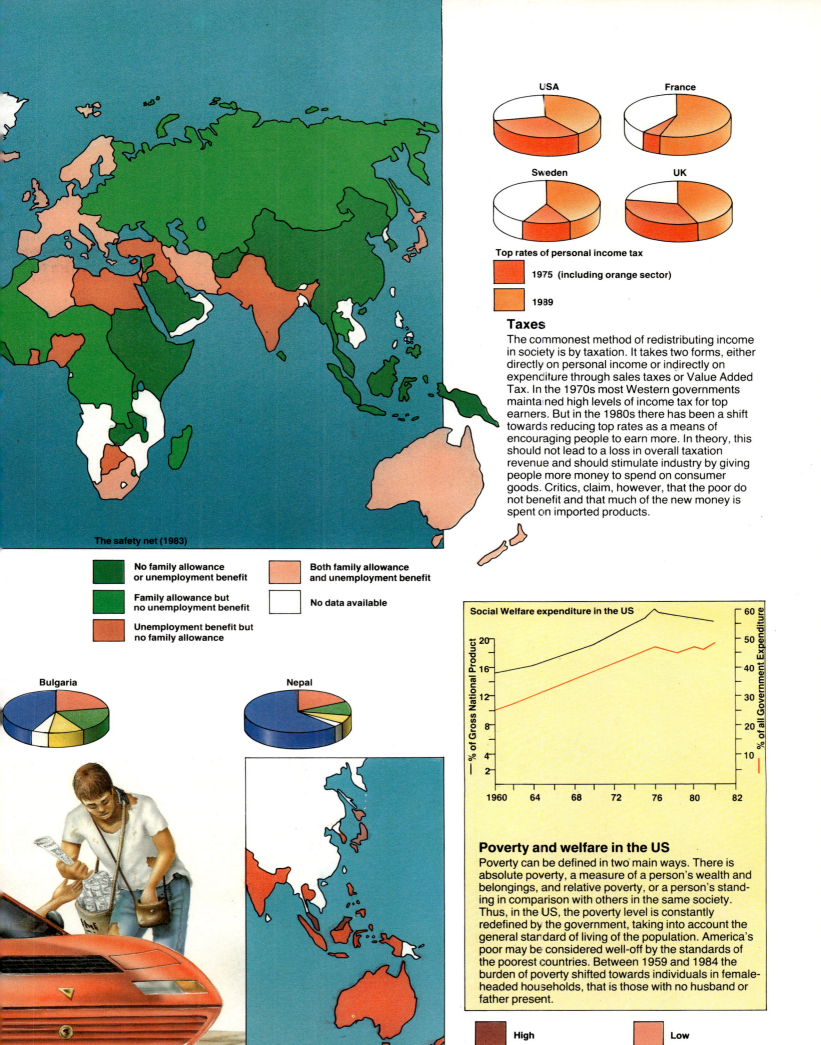

USA

France

Sweden

UK

Top rates of personal income tax

■ 1975 (including orange sector)

■ 1989

Taxes

The commonest method of redistributing income in society is by taxation. It takes two forms, either directly on personal income or indirectly on expenditure through sales taxes or Value Added Tax. In the 1970s most Western governments maintained high levels of income tax for top earners. But in the 1980s there has been a shift towards reducing top rates as a means of encouraging people to earn more. In theory, this should not lead to a loss in overall taxation revenue and should stimulate industry by giving people more money to spend on consumer goods. Critics, claim, however, that the poor do not benefit and that much of the new money is spent on imported products.

The safety net (1983)

■ No family allowance or unemployment benefit

■ Family allowance but no unemployment benefit

■ Unemployment benefit but no family allowance

■ Both family allowance and unemployment benefit

□ No data available

Bulgaria

Nepal

Social Welfare expenditure in the US

— % of Gross National Product

% of all Government Expenditure

1960   64   68   72   76   80   82

Poverty and welfare in the US

Poverty can be defined in two main ways. There is absolute poverty, a measure of a person's wealth and belongings, and relative poverty, or a person's standing in comparison with others in the same society. Thus, in the US, the poverty level is constantly redefined by the government, taking into account the general standard of living of the population. America's poor may be considered well-off by the standards of the poorest countries. Between 1959 and 1984 the burden of poverty shifted towards individuals in female-headed households, that is those with no husband or father present.

■ High

■ Medium

■ Low

□ No data available

19

8 Out of Work

In 1929 the world's economy was plunged into the Great Depression. Three years later up to 20% of the workforce of the industrialized countries was out of work, and industrial production was halved. Western governments responded with policies of full employment and schemes were introduced to protect the jobless. These worked until the 1970s, when once again the threat of long-term mass unemployment arose, calling for new and imaginative responses.

In societies where one's status and welfare depend on one's work, unemployment is a grave social issue. It has been linked to psychological distress, higher levels of anxiety, aggression and suicide. The social costs of unemployment include the loss of tax revenue, increased social security and health expenditure. Unemployment is often geographically concentrated, leading to the decline of entire communities. High unemployment has also been linked with social unrest and crime. Therefore, governments of quite different political persuasions have often placed joblessness high on their list of priorities.

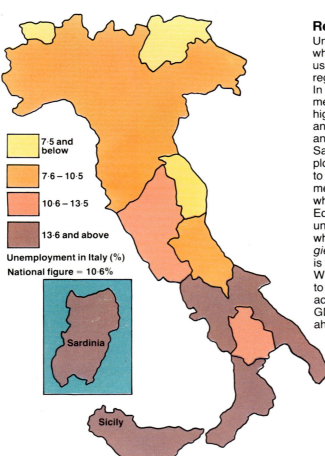

7·5 and below

7·6 – 10·5

10·6 – 13·5

13·6 and above

Unemployment in Italy (%)
National figure = 10·6%

Sardinia

Sicily

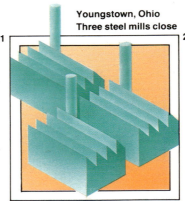

Youngstown, Ohio
Three steel mills close

1977 Loss of 4,000 jobs
1980 Loss of 3,500 jobs
1980 Loss of 1,400 jobs

Loss of up to 14,000 jobs due to domino effect

De-industrialization

Western countries are experiencing declining levels of manufacturing employment while manufacturers comprise an ever smaller share of total economic activity. This process of 'de-industrialization' has struck hardest in communities with narrow economic bases, for example those dependent on steel, mining, and port-based industry. The sequence diagram is based on the example of Youngstown, Ohio, and suggests how the effect of plant closure ripples through a community. When a large plant closes, not only do its workers lose out, but there is a knock-on effect on the suppliers and sub-contractors, local shops, and the housing market.

Regional unemployment

Unemployment rarely affects whole countries equally, and is usually concentrated in certain regions or even parts of regions. In Italy, for example, unemployment rates have long been higher in the more agricultural and less industrialized south, and in outlying regions such as Sardinia and Sicily. The unemployment figures, however, tend to conceal seasonal employment in agriculture and tourism, which is difficult to assess. Equally, they also fail to include undeclared or clandestine work, which in Italy is known as *arrangiersi* or 'fixing' work, work that is hidden from the authorities. When the government decided to include an estimate of such activity as part of its official GDP, it rose by 15%, putting it ahead of Britain and France.

Lower incomes from redundancy payments or re-employment at lower wages

Falling sales of new cars and other good more jobs lost

Higher levels of anxiety, aggression, alcoholism and other forms of stress

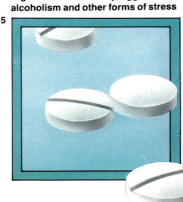

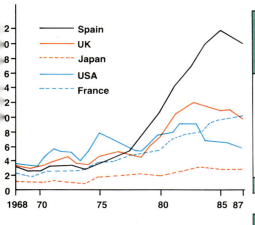

Spain
UK
Japan
USA
France

1968 70   75   80   85 87

Proportion of unemployed

USA France Japan UK Italy

aged 55 and over   aged 15–24 (1987)

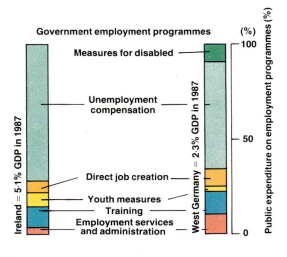

Government employment programmes   (%)

Measures for disabled

Unemployment compensation

Direct job creation

Youth measures

Training

Employment services and administration

Ireland = 5·1% GDP in 1987

West Germany = 2·3% GDP in 1987

Public expenditure on employment programmes (%)

An era of mass unemployment?

In the 1960s unemployment levels in the developed world were generally low with very little difference between countries. But the combined effects of the 1973–74 and 1980–83 recessions have resulted not only in much higher levels but also greater international variations. Levels have fallen in North America and Scandinavia, but remain high in southern Europe. Some experts now believe that industrialized economies can never achieve the goal of full employment, and that societies must learn to adjust to permanent high unemployment.

Young and old

Unemployment has been persistently higher among both the young and the old over recent years. In 1986, 5 million of the EEC's 13.5 million unemployed were under 25 years of age, the hardest hit being children of migrant workers, the disabled, and those living in depressed industrial regions. Many young unemployed are removed from the official figures by being placed in youth training schemes. Older workers often find that their skills are no longer needed but are unable to migrate to find new work.

Government response

Governments can rise and fall on the basis of their response to unemployment. Some such as the UK rely on indirect policies designed to create the right climate for economic growth. Others emphasize direct policies, which may be passive (income maintenance) or active (job creation and training). Canada, Sweden, and West Germany devote huge resources to placement services, helping the unemployed to find work. Belgium specializes in direct job creation by channelling the unemployed into the public sector.

Proportion of GNP spent on labour market programmes

4% and over   1–2·5%   Less than 1%

2·5–3·9%

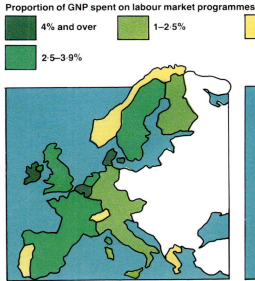

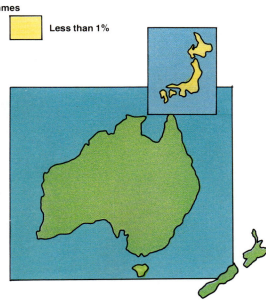

Increase in domestic court cases, child abuse and neglect

6

Crime rates up 6–8% in two years

7

Some relocation but most stay to find other jobs

8

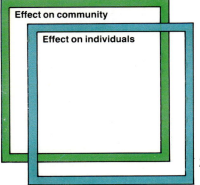

Effect on community

Effect on individuals

9 Shelter

Shelter is a basic need. Not only does it afford protection from the elements and a place to keep one's possessions, but it may also be a source of savings and wealth. Warm, dry housing is also necessary for a person's mental and physical health. Throughout the world, access to housing is a sign of status, a source of inequality and a major social division.

There are many ways of obtaining shelter, but each seems to have its own limitations. These fall into two categories: quantity and quality. In poorer countries there are often shortages of dwellings, attributable to low personal incomes on the one hand and a lack of public capital on the other. In wealthier countries housing problems mainly concern the quality of accommodation.

How each country solves these problems depends upon their separate economic and political characters. As housing comes to represent an increasing share of individual and national wealth, the shelter issue is sure to gain in importance.

Slums in the sky
After 1945 many governments undertook the rapid construction of mass housing. In developing countries such projects were designed to house growing urban populations cheaply, while in the developed world they were aimed at not only reducing housing shortages but also rehousing people displaced by slum clearances. Many such projects proved unpopular with their residents. Rapid construction with cheap materials produced many design flaws. In St. Louis, Missouri, the Pruitt-Igoe project won an architectural award when it was designed in 1951. By 1972 the costs of repairing the vandalized and collapsing buildings had risen so much that it was cheaper for the authorities to blow the project u

Accommodation in selected European countries

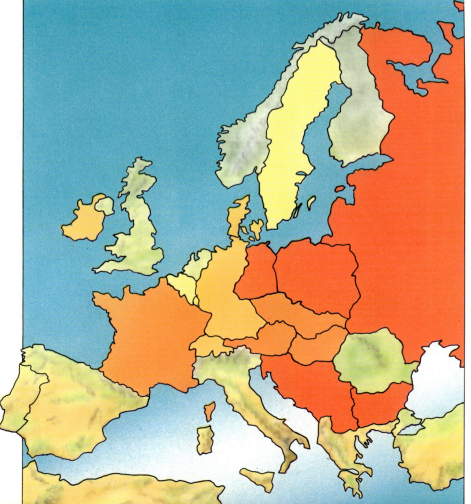

■	50–69
■	70–89
■	90–109
■	110 and over

Useful floor space per dwelling (sq. m.)

State provision
Socialist governments are generally committed to providing housing for all their citizens through control of construction and allocation. In Eastern Europe, for example, there are four main sources of accommodation: state-owned dwellings, units built by factories for their employees, workers' cooperatives, and a small private market. Slow-growing economies have meant that in the past housing in such countries has received a low priority. The result is an inadequate level of provision and often the richer people get the newer, better dwellings. To reduce the problem, many Eastern European countries are now promoting a private market.

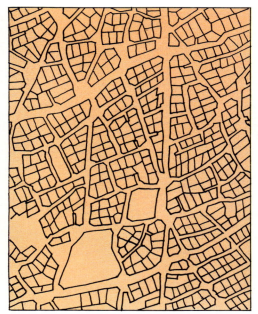

Planning for the community

Old Naledi is an example of a 'regularized' shanty settlement. Situated outside Gaborone, Botswana, the layout of the settlement has evolved in a haphazard manner according to the needs of the community, in preference to an imposed grid pattern common in North American cities.

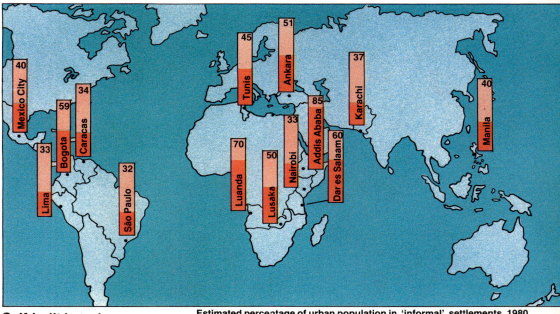

Estimated percentage of urban population in 'informal' settlements, 1980

Self-built housing

Where people cannot afford to buy homes and there is no alternative, they may construct their own. Many people in the cities of the developing world inhabit 'shanty' settlements. Governments are now beginning to recognize the advantages of helping the poor house themselves. Given time and money, self-built dwellings may become sound structures and the communities may rig up water and electricity supplies. The World Bank encourages upgrading by advancing funds. Such 'regularized' settlements may, however, become too expensive for newcomers; a recent UN report concluded that very few housing programmes helped the poorest tenth of the urban population.

Homelessness

There are homeless people in every country, though rarely is it known exactly how many. In Cairo 1 million people live in cemeteries, while in Calcutta 600,000 sleep on the streets. The US has 1 million homeless people, the countries of the EEC up to 1.5 million, and the UK officially has 112,000. Although poverty is the root cause of homelessness everywhere, a contributory factor in both the US and the UK is thought to be the discharging of patients from mental health institutions. Today, there are more youths, women, and children among the homeless than ever before.

10 Women at work

According to a statement made by the United Nations Conference on Women in 1980, women worldwide make up one-third of the official labour force, work two-thirds of all working hours, provide 44% of the world's food supply, but receive only one-tenth of the world's income and own 1% of the world's property.

Women workers suffer a double disadvantage. They are either unpaid or poorly paid. Their low income makes it easy for employers to exploit them. They also have the responsibility of child-rearing.

Yet in the developed world more and more women are entering the workforce, either as a means of economic independence or to increase family income. In newly industrializing countries cheap female labour is often used in labour-intensive industries. Women in agricultural societies have the hardest lives, many coping on their own, the men having migrated in search of better wages. Basic daily tasks such as fetching water and fuelwood or grinding grain can take several hours and consume a lot of physical energy. Misguided development policies often leave them relatively worse off by channelling jobs and income to men.

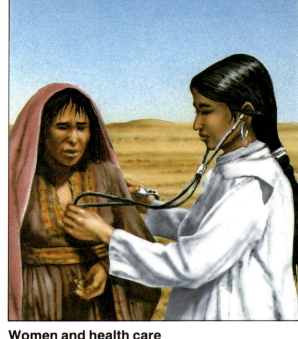

Women and health care
In many countries, the majority of employees in the health services are women, particularly so amongst the nursing profession. In the USSR, an above-average proportion of doctors are women. In some developing countries, such as Pakistan, women can provide essential basic health care. Although they are never awarded the status of doctors, they are known as 'barefoot doctors', and their work saves lives.

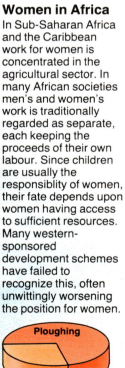

Women in Africa
In Sub-Saharan Africa and the Caribbean work for women is concentrated in the agricultural sector. In many African societies men's and women's work is traditionally regarded as separate, each keeping the proceeds of their own labour. Since children are usually the responsiblity of women, their fate depends upon women having access to sufficient resources. Many western-sponsored development schemes have failed to recognize this, often unwittingly worsening the position for women.

Male

Female

Domestic chores

Processing/storing crops

Weeding

Planting

Ploughing

Harvesting

Caring for livestock

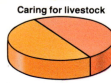

Division of labour in rural Africa

24

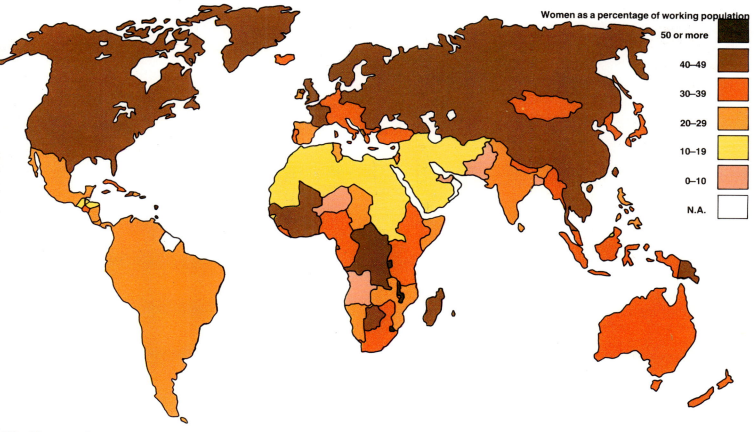

Women as a percentage of working population

⬛	50 or more
🟫	40–49
🟧	30–39
🟧	20–29
🟨	10–19
🟧	0–10
⬜	N.A.

Working mothers

The responsibility for having and raising children prevents many women from working outside the home and pursuing a career. Governments can help by providing rights to paid leave and child care facilities. Levels of such provision vary considerably. In Sweden, where 76% of women work, mothers receive six weeks off before birth and 18 months afterwards, and fathers also get time off, something which is not available in any other country. By contrast, in Japan a woman can be expected to resign if she becomes pregnant. In many countries not all women qualify for maternity rights; in Britain a woman is eligible only if she has been continuously employed in the same company for two years, which rules out over half of all female workers.

'Women's Work'

Where women work outside the home they are usually concentrated in a few industries and occupations. Worldwide these include nursing, teaching and child-care. There are also national specialisms. In the US bank tellers and in the UK secretaries and office cleaners tend to be women. Domestic service is the lot of the majority of women in Latin America, but in Africa they specialize in agriculture, and in South-East Asia are concentrated in textiles and electronics assembly. Conservative attitudes in Islamic countries restrict working women generally to all-female institutions, such as hospitals and schools.

Unequal pay

With the Equal Pay Act of 1963, the United States led the world in calling for fair wages in employment regardless of sex. Now more than 90 countries have such legislation – but nowhere in the world is such a policy enforced. Globally, on average, women receive 73¢ to every $1 earned by men; at best (in Sweden) the ratio is 80¢ to $1, at worst (in Korea) it is 50¢ to $1. In the US, a female secretary with 18 years' experience receives a salary less than that of an unskilled male parking lot attendant. Even among graduates of Harvard Business School, women earn $6,000–12,000 less than their male counterparts.

	Weeks off	at % of salary
Britain	18	90
France	46	90
Italy	48	80
Spain	14	75
Sweden	84	90
West Germany	26	100

11 Migrant labour

The movement of people between continents and regions has been a characteristic of human history, creating new and diverse societies. Nearly 8 million Africans were transported from their homes in the slave trade of the 17th and 18th centuries. The 19th century was an era of colonization and settlement, as Europeans occupied the New World. In modern times this immigration of families to new countries has given way to another phenomenon: migrant labour.

Since World War II governments have acted to stem permanent settlement and have begun instead to accept temporary workers to suit their needs for labour. There are now some 25–30 million migrants working outside their home territories. These workers fill labour shortages and help rebuild economies, often accepting jobs that others would not consider. Throughout the developed world such jobs are often the worst paid, physically demanding, unskilled, and sometimes involve working in hazardous conditions.

In the 1970s recession created the conditions for a backlash against these guest-workers, forcing many governments to attempt to control numbers. This reaction coincided with a period in which many young male migrants were raising families and becoming more permanent members of their adopted societies. In France, Norway and Denmark political parties advocating anti-immigrant legislation have begun to gain ground.

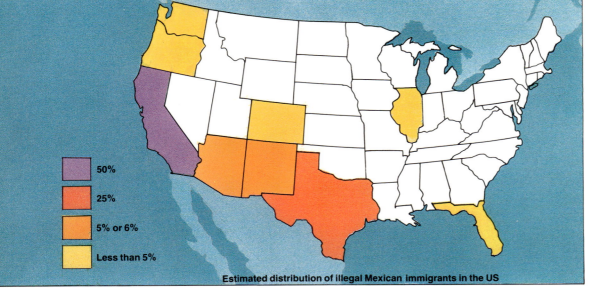

Estimated distribution of illegal Mexican immigrants in the US

50%	
25%	
5% or 6%	
Less than 5%	

Needed but not wanted

The considerable national and state-initiated efforts to control unofficial migration from Mexico into the USA have proved largely ineffective. It is thought that there are between one and two million Mexicans resident in the USA who are breaking immigration laws. Despite complaints that the so-called 'illegals' are taking jobs away from citizens and placing a burden on social services, it is likely that these workers contribute more to the economy than they take from it. Without their cheap labour, Americans would pay more for food, restaurant meals, clothes, electronics and other goods. Many argue that the only way to halt migrant labour is to assist Mexico's economic growth.

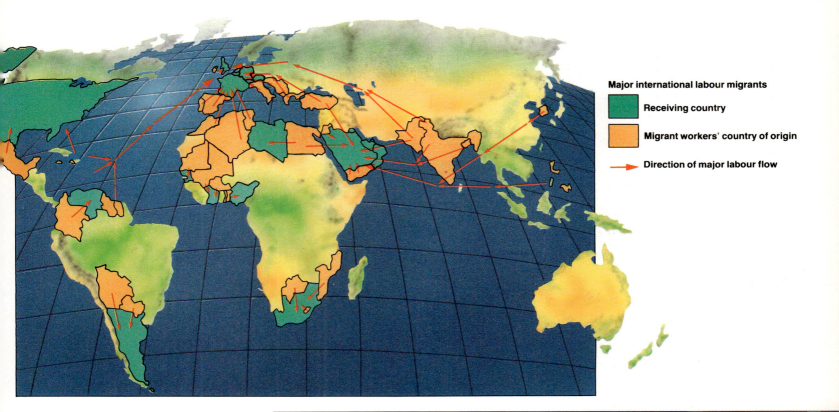

Major international labour migrants

■ Receiving country

■ Migrant workers' country of origin

→ Direction of major labour flow

Sending savings home

The migrant's goal is to make as much money as possible in the shortest period of time. Usually, most of this money is sent home to the family while the migrant keeps only enough for basic subsistence. The funds returned by migrants, called remittances, amount to vast sums and often comprise a substantial portion of some countries' foreign earnings. (Examples below indicate amounts returned in one year and their value relative to export earnings.) Developing countries badly need such money to service their foreign debts and some, like India and Pakistan, provide emigrants with special tax exemptions and deposit accounts encouraging them to return their earnings from abroad.

Xenophobia

With the influx of a large number of workers from other countries there often arises among the receiving population the phenomenon of xenophobia, or fear of foreigners. This may take various forms, from a mild dislike of the newcomers, to prejudice and discrimination in services, to outright racism expressed in violence. Furthermore, as economies decline, blame is often unfairly placed on the immigrants. Since 1981 there have been 160 racially motivated killings in France, and in 1985 in one London suburb alone there were 112 racist attacks. Both France and Britain have seen the rise of neo-fascist political groups who argue for racial purity and call for the expulsion of immigrants.

Oil boom workers

The states of the Arab Gulf experienced a massive growth in labour immigration over a relatively brief period. Beginning in the early 1970s, when the world price of oil quadrupled, these countries were injected with vast amounts of new income. With such capital they embarked upon development projects centred on the construction of new physical infrastructures, such as roads and dams. These projects demanded a large quantity of unskilled manual labour. In 1970 the number of migrant workers in these countries totalled 660,000; by 1985 it stood at over 5 million. Most migrants come from other Arab nations, though many come from South and East Asia. In some of the Gulf States, the migrants outnumber the local citizens.

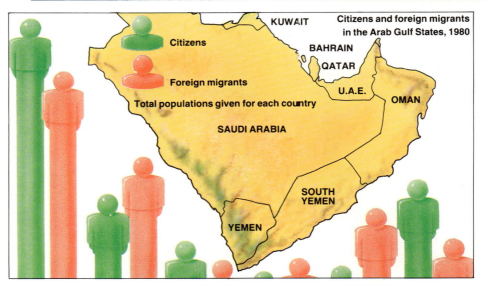

Citizens and foreign migrants in the Arab Gulf States, 1980

Citizens

Foreign migrants

Total populations given for each country

KUWAIT
BAHRAIN
QATAR
U.A.E.
OMAN
SAUDI ARABIA
SOUTH YEMEN
YEMEN

Saudi Arabia 7,235,000
Kuwait 1,355,827
Bahrain 358,875
Qatar 200,000
U.A.E. 557,887
Oman 900,000

12 Health care

Health care is one of a society's most vital resources, and yet throughout the world it is in crisis. In developing countries imported drugs may consume up to half the health budget. In the west, ageing populations and rising expectations are putting pressure on both individual and government finances.

State-funded health care was first introduced by Germany in 1883, and since then it has been a cornerstone of the Western welfare state. In Britain and Italy the health care system is centrally run and funded by compulsory social insurance payments by workers and employers. The British system is based upon the principle that health care should be available to all regardless of an individual's wealth. In the US, the burden of financing health care falls upon the individual. France mixes both forms, with a basic level of care provided by the state and an option to spend more by contributing to work-based mutual or cooperative organizations.

None of the above appears to be perfect and governments are trying to learn from each other in a widespread phase of health care reform. What is clear, is that the countries which spend the most do not necessarily have the healthiest populations. This is because the general level of health is more dependent on good nutrition, a clean environment, sound housing and the absence of poverty, rather than upon the number of hospitals or doctors.

Too many or not enough?
The average number of people served by each physician varies from over 88,000 in Ethiopia to 270 in the USSR. But more doctors do not necessarily mean a better health care system. Many Western countries now think that they have too many doctors and are trying to limit the number of medical students. The USSR is particularly notorious for the inefficiency of its health service. Of greater worry in the developed world is the problem of finding enough teenagers to become nurses, which is often a low-paid job with long hours.

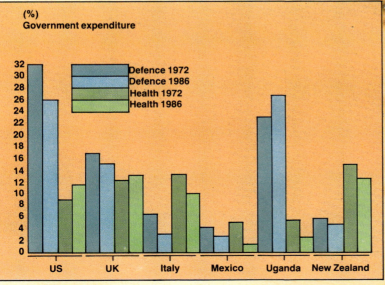

(%)
Government expenditure

Defence 1972
Defence 1986
Health 1972
Health 1986

32
30
28
26
24
22
20
18
16
14
12
10
8
6
4
2
0

US   UK   Italy   Mexico   Uganda   New Zealand

A matter of life or death?
Most governments and their electorates face a choice between spending on health and other areas of national interest, such as defence. Attempts to cut health spending have almost brought down governments in Ireland and the Netherlands in recent years and, in general, defence is losing out to health care. Some poorer countries, such as Uganda, are obliged to control civil unrest, diverting resources away from health care while others, notably the US, have assumed global responsibilities which are difficult to relinquish. But one-fifteenth of the world's annual expenditure on defence would easily provide enough resources for primary health care throughout the world.

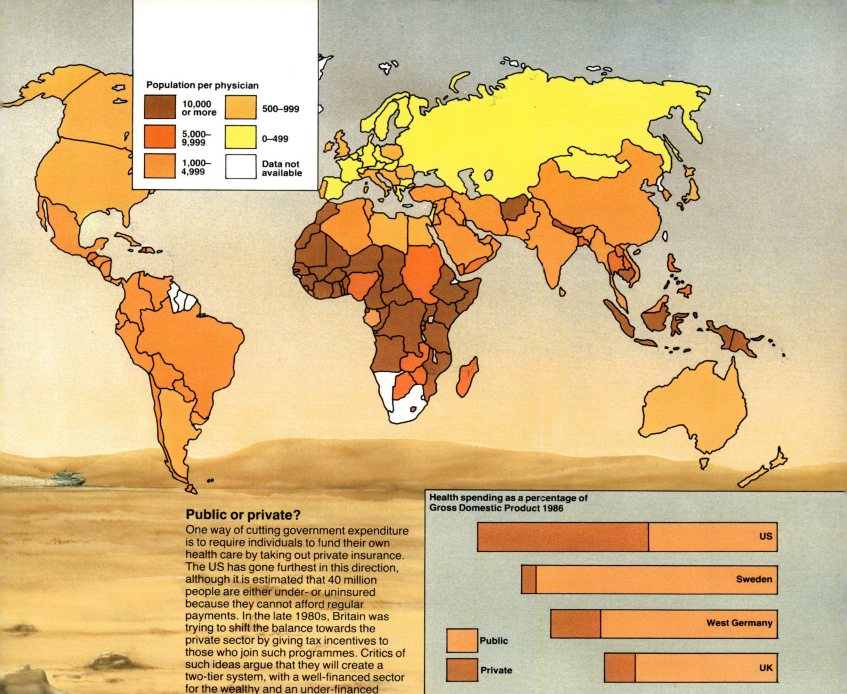

Population per physician

- 10,000 or more
- 5,000–9,999
- 1,000–4,999
- 500–999
- 0–499
- Data not available

Public or private?

One way of cutting government expenditure is to require individuals to fund their own health care by taking out private insurance. The US has gone furthest in this direction, although it is estimated that 40 million people are either under- or uninsured because they cannot afford regular payments. In the late 1980s, Britain was trying to shift the balance towards the private sector by giving tax incentives to those who join such programmes. Critics of such ideas argue that they will create a two-tier system, with a well-financed sector for the wealthy and an under-financed sector for everyone else.

Health spending as a percentage of Gross Domestic Product 1986

- Public
- Private

	US
	Sweden
	West Germany
	UK

12 10 8 6 4 2 0

Oral rehydration therapy

Infant diarrhoea is easy and cheap to prevent. In 1978 the World Health Organization launched a programme of oral rehydration therapy. By 1989 it planned to make oral rehydration salts, which are packets of salts which help bodies absorb and retain fluids, available to 80% of the children in 126 countries. Such packets are not only cheap, but they may be made locally, thus sparing the expense of importing expensive foreign medicines. Some controversy surrounds the continued attempts of multi-national chemical and medicine companies to persuade people to buy their compounds instead of these cheap alternatives.

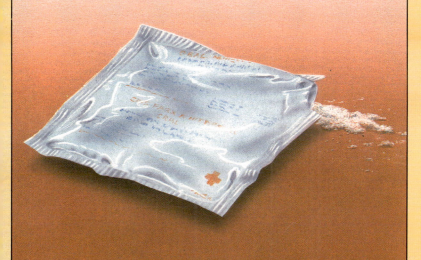

Health care for the developing world

Poorer countries generally spend a lower proportion of their wealth on health care than richer countries. But investing in primary health care rather than in more doctors and hospitals is cheaper and can often bring greater good. This includes investment in safe water, immunization, the monitoring of diseases and health education. There is also room for traditional medicine. Three-quarters of the world's disease is preventable through such simple low-cost methods.

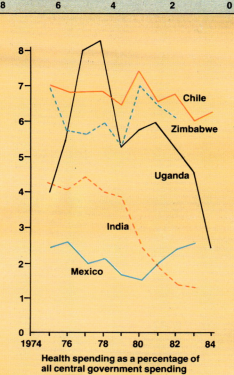

Chile
Zimbabwe
Uganda
India
Mexico

1974 76 78 80 82 84

Health spending as a percentage of all central government spending

13 Famine

Famine and hunger have recurred throughout human history, often accompanying natural disasters and wars. It is estimated that in the 1930s 20–30% of the population of Western Europe was malnourished and two-thirds of the world's population was underfed. Recent improvements in agricultural technology together with an expansion in cultivated area has reduced that proportion to perhaps one-quarter. But, although there are now fewer famines which occur in fewer parts of the world, when they do occur more people suffer, due to increasing population numbers.

Famine should be distinguished from undernourishment (or the lack of certain types of nutrition), which may occur in any society. Famine refers to an event when these conditions reach epidemic or crisis proportions and threaten the viability of a social system because of widespread death, migration or economic collapse. Although it may be triggered by a natural event such as drought or flooding, it is the economic and political nature of the society itself which determines whether famine occurs or not in such circumstances. War (as in Mozambique), landlessness (as in Northeast Brazil) and governmental neglect (as in Ethiopia) all contribute to the situation. Whole societies rarely suffer, and it is usually those with the least to offer in return for food, such as the poor, the landless and those without relatives, who suffer most.

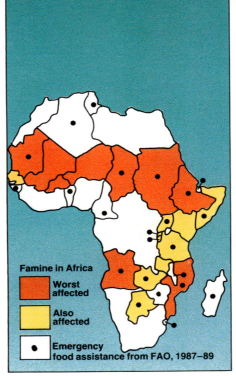

Famine in Africa
- Worst affected
- Also affected
- Emergency food assistance from FAO, 1987–89

The threat of famine

Although famine is hard to define, the UN's Food and Agriculture Organization now has an extensive monitoring and early warning system. It regularly defines countries where there are abnormal food shortages which require exceptional assistance. The FAO also gives emergency food assistance, often helping to redistribute local surpluses within a country.

Food aid in cereals

Food aid accounts for 5% of the world's trade in food. In 1974 the World Food Conference set a minimum target of 10 million tonnes of food aid annually. 10 years later, in response to the African crisis, this target was finally achieved. Western countries are the major donors, and Egypt, Bangladesh, Sri Lanka, Pakistan and Ethiopia the major recipients. Critics of food aid say that it depresses the prices received by local farmers and discourages domestic agriculture. They also argue that it is often used for political ends, to reward some countries and punish others.

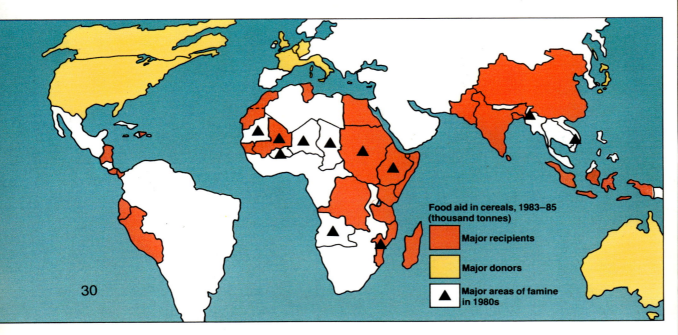

Food aid in cereals, 1983–85 (thousand tonnes)
- Major recipients
- Major donors
- Major areas of famine in 1980s

Bangladesh: 1974

Bangladesh is a mostly low-lying country through which the Ganges and Brahmaputra rivers flow. The coastal areas are subject to frequent typhoons. In 1974 the Brahmaputra flooded and destroyed two of the year's rice crops in a large part of the country. Although 1974 was still a record harvest year, in many of the areas worst hit between 24,000 and 100,000 people died from famine. Those who died were mainly landless agricultural labourers who had nothing to exchange for food. Also, in 1974 the US cut off its food aid program because of Bangladesh's trade with Cuba, restoring it only after the famine had passed its worst.

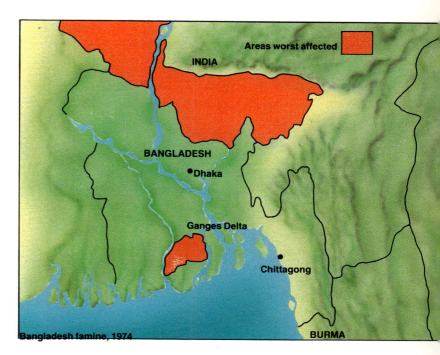

Bangladesh famine, 1974

Ethiopia

Ethiopia has a population of 40 million and an average annual income of less that £100 per person. Because the lowlands are too dry for arable farming, and the highlands experience severe soil erosion drought is a recurrent problem.

But the environment alone does not explain the recurrence of famine. In recent years, wars fought between the government and separatist movements in Eritrea, Tigre, and the Ogaden have not only used up half the government's budget but have also created refugees and hampered relief efforts. Because the government tried to cover up the 1972—74 famines, and in 1984—85 was slow to respond, between 250,000 and 750,000 people died. When the rains returned many families had sold their ploughs, seeds or livestock and so were unable to take full advantage.

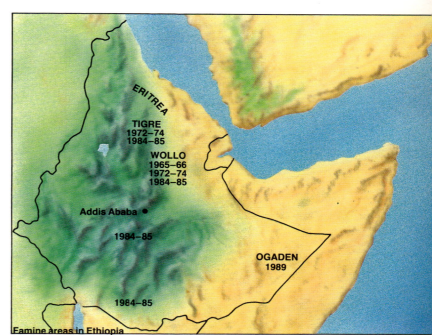

Famine areas in Ethiopia

Food production in Africa

In 1985 the Food and Agricultural Organization of the UN identified 20 African nations experiencing food shortages. In a normal year up to 100 million people may be malnourished. African agriculture faces environmental constraints – 80% of the soils have fertility limitations and 50% of the continent is too dry to support rain-fed agriculture. In addition, governments have all too often neglected investment in agriculture. Investment in food crops has been especially low. Cash crops which are for export have had more investment, but low world prices for such crops, together with an insupportable debt burden have not helped the situation. Finally, Africa's population is growing at roughly 3% per year. Therefore, although Africa's food production is rising by 2% per year, since the 1970s production per person has been falling, unlike every other continent.

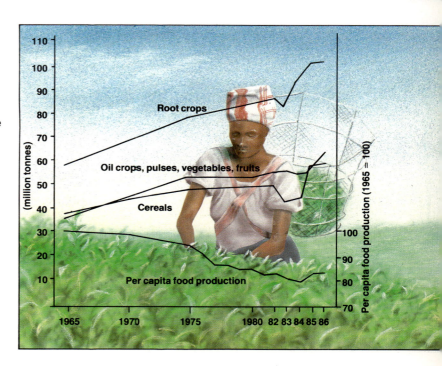

14 Mental health

Between 5 and 15% of the world's population is estimated to suffer emotional or personality disorders. In Britain, one in twelve men and one in eight women will have psychiatric treatment at some time in their lives. In the US 15% of the population is afflicted by psychological disorders each year. $23.5 billion is spent annually on mental health care. Mental health and mental illness represent major issues for all human societies but there is no agreement as to their definition or treatment.

Mental health and mental illness are usually considered to be distinct from mental retardation or mental disorders caused by genetic or acquired damage to the central nervous system. Definitions of mental health are cultural, involving accepted notions of what are normal thoughts and behaviours. Mentally healthy people are expected to be able to cope with or adjust to changing circumstances or life stages, such as adolescence or menopause. Mental illness is regarded as when individuals appear to behave in an abnormal way.

Modern treatment in Western countries includes psychiatric therapy and counselling. Social and environmental factors, such as overcrowding, noise, crime and poor housing which have been shown to contribute to mental illness, are considered to be much harder to treat.

Suicide

If mental illness is defined as thinking and behaving differently to the accepted norm, then suicide is perhaps its most extreme form. Occurring more in cities, among single people, and among men (three to five times more than women, globally), suicide is caused by a wide variety of factors. Most psychologists attribute suicide to 'alienation' meaning lack of integration with other people, or to problems of coping with radical life changes or pressures. Even in Europe, suicide rates vary greatly, including some of the highest levels in the world. Canada, Mexico and Panama are among those countries with the lowest officially recorded levels.

Mental illness among the affluent

Many US states with high levels of mental illness are also those where people move home most frequently. It is possible that mental illness is a particular affliction of the mobile and affluent middle-classes, members of whom have come to be indifferent to community participation.

Levels of mental illness 1965–70

High
Above average
Below average
Low

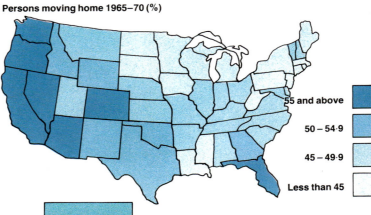

Persons moving home 1965–70 (%)

55 and above
50 – 54·9
45 – 49·9
Less than 45

Suicide rates in Europe

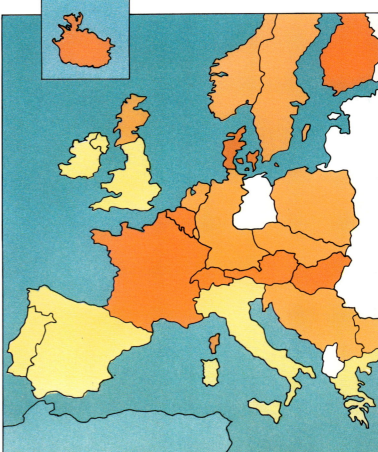

Suicides per 100,000 inhabitants

30 and above
20 – 29
10 – 19
Less than 10
Figures not available

Historical trends

Societies have treated the mentally ill differently through the ages. In medieval times serious mental disorders were thought to be signs of demonic possession. In the 17th and 18th centuries the mentally ill were considered to be wicked because they were idle. They were confined under severe conditions in asylums. In the early 20th century, psychologists like Sigmund Freud emphasized that there were unconscious roots to most mental disturbances, and that they could be treated through analysis. By the 1960s, pharmaceutical drugs were used to treat some forms of mental illness, and this, combined with the shift to community health care, led to a decline in the number of hospitalized mental patients.

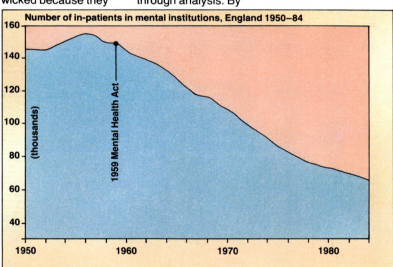

Number of in-patients in mental institutions, England 1950–84

(y-axis: 40, 60, 80, 100, 120, 140, 160 (thousands))

1959 Mental Health Act

(x-axis: 1950, 1960, 1970, 1980)

De-institution-alization

Until only 20 years ago, society endeavoured to keep 'out of sight' those individuals who were considered 'out of mind'. Since the late 1950s more mentally ill people have been treated within local communities. In the United Kingdom in 1959 and in the United States in 1963, legislative acts were passed to promote community care facilities for the mentally ill; the idea was to save money on hospitals while giving patients a therapeutic social environment. A huge decline among the number of in-patients in mental hospitals and wards has resulted. Today, fewer people are admitted or readmitted to mental hospitals. 50% of mental patients live with their families, 25% under supervision with non-relatives, 15% alone, and the balance in a variety of usually unsupervised conditions. Community care may be therapeutic, but many persons often live far from out-patient facilities, and a large number go without any treatment or care – sometimes ending up homeless. It has been estimated that some 10,000 mentally ill people live on the streets of New York City.

Some types of mental disorder

Degenerative disorders deterioration of brain tissue affecting intellectual and motor abilities; aging, drug abuse, and alcoholism can cause this

Schizophrenia a broad term used to describe types of extreme disorder in mood, thinking, behaviour, perceptions and emotions

Psychosis severe disturbance of mental state characterized by apparent loss of contact with reality

Anxiety disorders and neurosis a range of disorders characterized by uncontrollable or inexplicable fear (*phobia*) or mental disruption caused by internal conflicts

Personality disorders prolonged abnormal behaviour usually caused by inability to adjust to social situations; includes such categories as: *paranoid* (unwarranted suspicion and distrust) *schizoid* (excessively introverted, seclusive) *histrionic* (exaggerated emotions) *narcissistic* (grandiose self-importance)

15 Heart Disease

Cardiovascular diseases are those which affect the heart and the blood vessels. They include ischaemic or coronary heart disease (CHD), cerebro-vascular disease or stroke, hypertension or high blood pressure, arterio-sclerosis and rheumatic heart disease. Together they form the major health threat to the developed world, with fatalities far exceeding any other single cause.

Because of its concentration in developed nations CHD was once thought to be a consequence of industrialization. However, international comparisons show that this may not be the case and medical opinion has suggested that diet may contribute to heart disease (although a costly 10-year medical trial designed to control diet among American males failed to produce the expected reduction in CHD). Another factor involved is hereditary. Men are more at risk than women, and CHD is most common among the 45–65 age group.

Having established some of the causes, it is now possible to educate populations about the risks and how to avoid them. Changing to more balanced diets, exercising and monitoring one's blood pressure can all help to reduce the Western world's most common killer. However, medical researchers have been forced to admit that the causes are far more complex than they once believed.

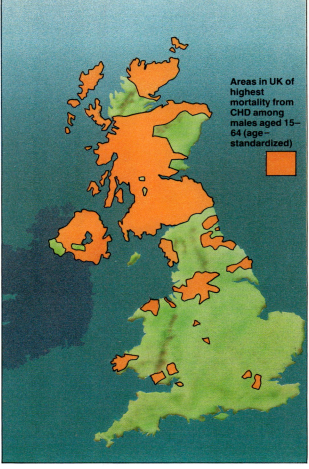

Areas in UK of highest mortality from CHD among males aged 15–64 (age-standardized)

The United Kingdom

Three of the top six countries in the CHD mortality table are part of the United Kingdom, while Ireland is fourth. CHD is the most frequent cause of mortality, accounting for one out of every three deaths in England and Wales. CHD is increasing in the UK, unlike the US or Australia. Its incidence is highest in Scotland and the industrial areas of the north, where poor diets coincide with the most vulnerable sectors of the population – males in semi-skilled and unskilled manual occupations, often living in sub-standard housing.

CHD mortality rate per 100,000 (age-standardized)			
	Male	Female	Total
Highest:			
N. Ireland	395	195	590
Finland	465	125	590
Scotland	395	195	590
Ireland	340	160	500
New Zealand	320	150	470
England and Wales	330	130	460
Lowest:			
Greece	130	40	170
Spain	140	30	170
France	120	20	140
Japan	60	20	80

Exercise

Physical activity lowers the risk of heart disease by reducing weight and keeping blood pressure at safe levels. But exercise must be regular. Irregular exertion can actually increase the likelihood of CHD, while exercise alone cannot ordinarily outweigh other factors such as poor diet or smoking. Some of the highest rates of heart disease in the world are among timber workers in Finland, who have very high rates of physical activity.

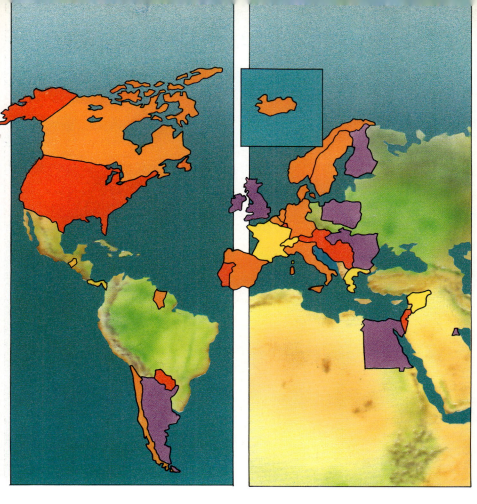

The map shows mortality rates for all cardio-vascular diseases for those few countries for which full data are available. Since the condition is most common among persons over 45, levels will be highest in countries with a higher proportion of their population in this age bracket. These figures have been standardized to present a truer comparison. Some countries have high rates of one of the family of diseases but low rates of another. Japan, for example, has low levels of CHD, but high levels of stroke, possibly due to regional diets which are high in salt content.

Mortality rate per 100,000

Colour	Rate
Purple	500 and above
Red	400 – 499
Orange	300 – 399
Yellow	299 and below

(Selected countries only reporting)

Diets most likely to cause CHD are those which contain foods high in saturated fats and have a low ratio of polyunsaturated to saturated fatty acids. A healthy diet is one which is balanced. During the Second World War the populations of the Scandinavian countries were obliged to eat foods with lower levels of saturated fats and the levels of heart disease fell drastically. Japan's low rate of heart disease may be attributed to a diet with lots of boiled rice, soup, vegetables, poultry and fish.

Foods higher in saturated fats		Foods lower in saturated fats	
Butter, lard, most margarines	Lamb, pork and beef	Low fat spreads, margarines high in poly-unsaturates	Skimmed or semi-skimmed milk
Cooking, coconut and palm oil	High fat cheeses, eg, cheddar	Corn, sunflower, safflower and soyabean oil	Fish, liver, chicken and turkey
Whole fat milk			Low fat cheeses, eg, Brie
			Fruit, vegetables and bread

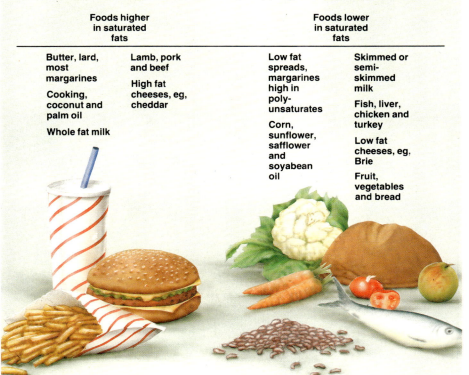

Drinking and smoking

Heart disease is a far greater problem than lung cancer for men who smoke. Giving up smoking greatly reduces the risk. The effects of alcohol are less direct; those who drink less are generally more likely to have healthy lifestyles. Those who drink excessively are more likely to have stressful lives, which can increase the risk of heart disease.

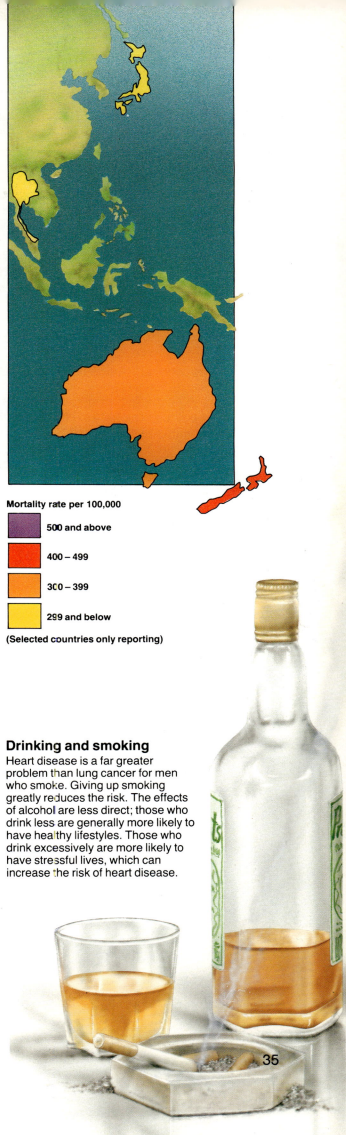

16 Alcoholism

In most countries of the world alcohol is a legal drug, but it is one which causes more sickness and deaths than any illegal drug. Alcoholism, or dependence upon alcohol, is associated with damage to the liver, some forms of cancer, possible foetal damage and a reduction in mental ability. Excessive drinking is thought to contribute to high levels of violence, anti-social behaviour, absenteeism from work and personal accidents.

Many governments regulate the sale of alcohol through setting licensing hours of drinking establishments, imposing high duties and taxes to raise its cost artificially or by banning its consumption outright. Some warn of the dangers of drinking and driving with expensive advertising campaigns. Yet none of these measures appears to have prevented the alarming rise in drinking among teenagers and young adults that is observed in the US and Europe.

Until recently alcoholics were scorned by society, making it difficult for them to admit to a problem and accept treatment. Now, however, especially in the US, much medical opinion suggests that alcoholism is a disease, and one which is partly connected to factors of inheritance. Like any other disease it can be treated medically. It seems important, therefore, that governments should not only warn of the dangers of alcohol, but should also inform public opinion about the disease, and help sufferers.

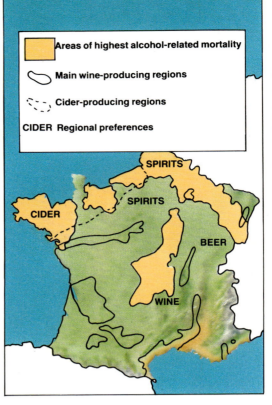

Areas of highest alcohol-related mortality

Main wine-producing regions

Cider-producing regions

CIDER Regional preferences

SPIRITS

SPIRITS

CIDER

BEER

WINE

Drinking in France
The French drink more alcohol than any other nation, although levels of consumption are now falling. Alcoholism causes one out of every 14 deaths, a half of all murders and a quarter of all suicides. However, fatalities are not highest in the main wine-producing regions, nor in the big cities. Britanny has the highest mortality rate, perhaps due to a long, though declining, tradition of private cider and apple-brandy making. The risk of death is highest among un-skilled workers and salaried farmers.

Cracking down
In many places there are restrictions on alcohol consumption. In Muslim countries it is banned altogether, and in many 'dry' counties of the US its sale is limited. When Mikhail Gorbachev became the leader of the Soviet Union he identified alcoholism as one of the country's most serious problems. It was contributing to falling levels of male life expectancy and low productivity at work. He cut vodka production, heavily reduced licensing hours, and banned alcohol from all official functions and public places. In France and many other countries alcohol advertising is banned from TV and cinema. Some governments are reluctant to take such drastic actions since duty and taxes on alcohol raise considerable sums. In Britain the £6 billion revenue from such sources is equivalent to a third of the cost of the National Health Service.

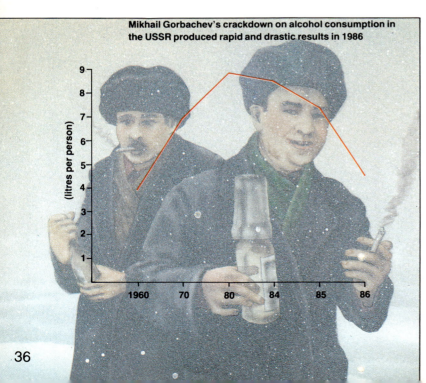

Mikhail Gorbachev's crackdown on alcohol consumption in the USSR produced rapid and drastic results in 1986

(litres per person)

9
8
7
6
5
4
3
2
1

1960   70   80   84   85   86

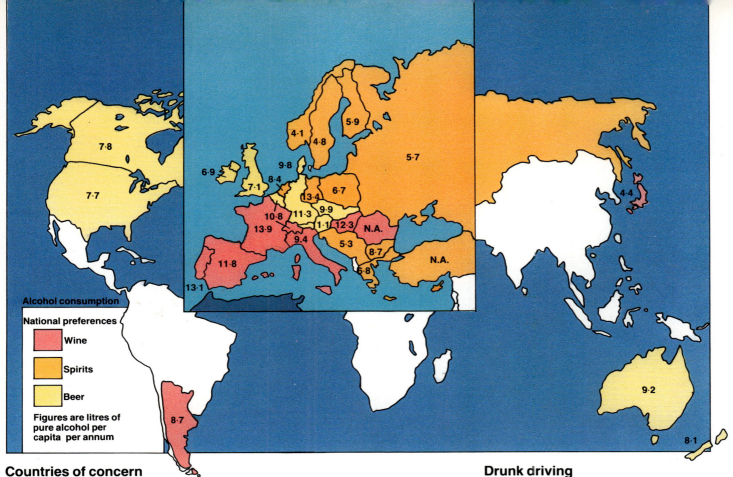

Alcohol consumption

National preferences

- 🟥 Wine
- 🟧 Spirits
- 🟨 Beer

Figures are litres of pure alcohol per capita per annum

Countries of concern

In Europe and North America levels of alcohol consumption peaked in the 19th century, declined from 1900, but then rose rapidly after 1945 as new types of drinkers, particularly women and teenagers, emerged. World beer production more than doubled between 1960 and 1980, with the USA, USSR, West Germany and the UK as the main producers. Beer accounts for two-thirds of all alcohol production.

The World Health Organization is concerned that in a few western countries alcohol consumption continues to rise, while many developing countries such as South Korea, Mexico and parts of Africa are starting to show an upwards trend. Drinking in these new countries is not, however, the result of international trade, but of domestic industry, particularly in beer. Many such countries will be unprepared for the social and medical costs of increased alcoholism.

Drunk driving

Drinking alcohol slows down reaction time, diminishes concentration, and reduces vision. Consequently drunk driving poses a major hazard, resulting in 24,000 deaths in the US (over half of the total of road deaths) and 950 deaths in Britain (1 out of every 5) in 1986. In Britain the legal limit of 80mg of alcohol per litre of blood is higher than in most of the US, Japan, Australia and Scandinavia. Even at that level, equivalent to 2 pints of beer for a male or 1 for a female, the risk of an accident is doubled. Although 100,000 people a year are caught over the limit, many people want more frequent testing of motorists and tougher penalties, including bans from driving for life.

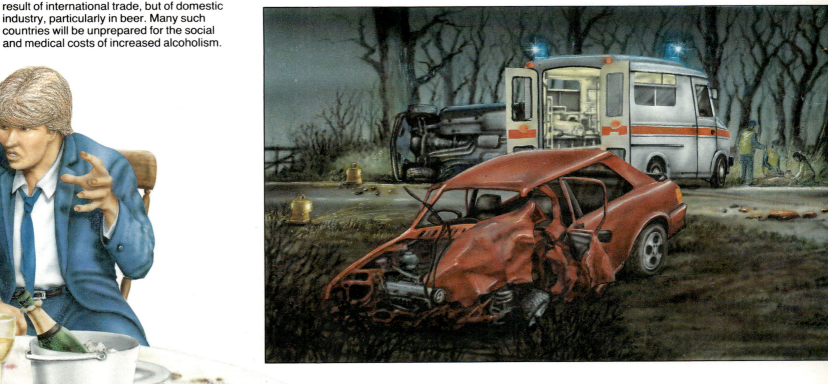

17 The Drugs Trade

Illegal drugs pose a global problem. They are not just a concern for those who are addicted to their effects, or the law enforcement officers who work to stop the sale and use of narcotics in their own countries. They have a significant impact on the world economy, international relations, and politics within both developing and developed countries. The underground trade in drugs such as heroin, cocaine, and cannabis has overtaken oil to become the world's second biggest business after arms sales. It is currently estimated that the trade amounts to £380 billion. In the United States alone, the illegal narcotics business is worth US$119 billion per year, more than the combined profits of the country's top 500 corporations.

Vast networks are involved in growing, harvesting, refining, transporting, and distributing the drugs. Yet these networks do not just consist of criminals and henchmen, but also peasants, businessmen, political terrorists and government officials.

Given the scale of business, fighting the drugs trade is extremely difficult if not impossible. Billions of pounds are spent around the world each year in an attempt to stamp it out. Yet the trade has continued to increase over the past two decades. Some people are now calling for a partial legalization of the less harmful drugs in order to concentrate resources on the harder varieties. Whatever happens, more cooperation between countries is necessary to monitor and break up this global traffic.

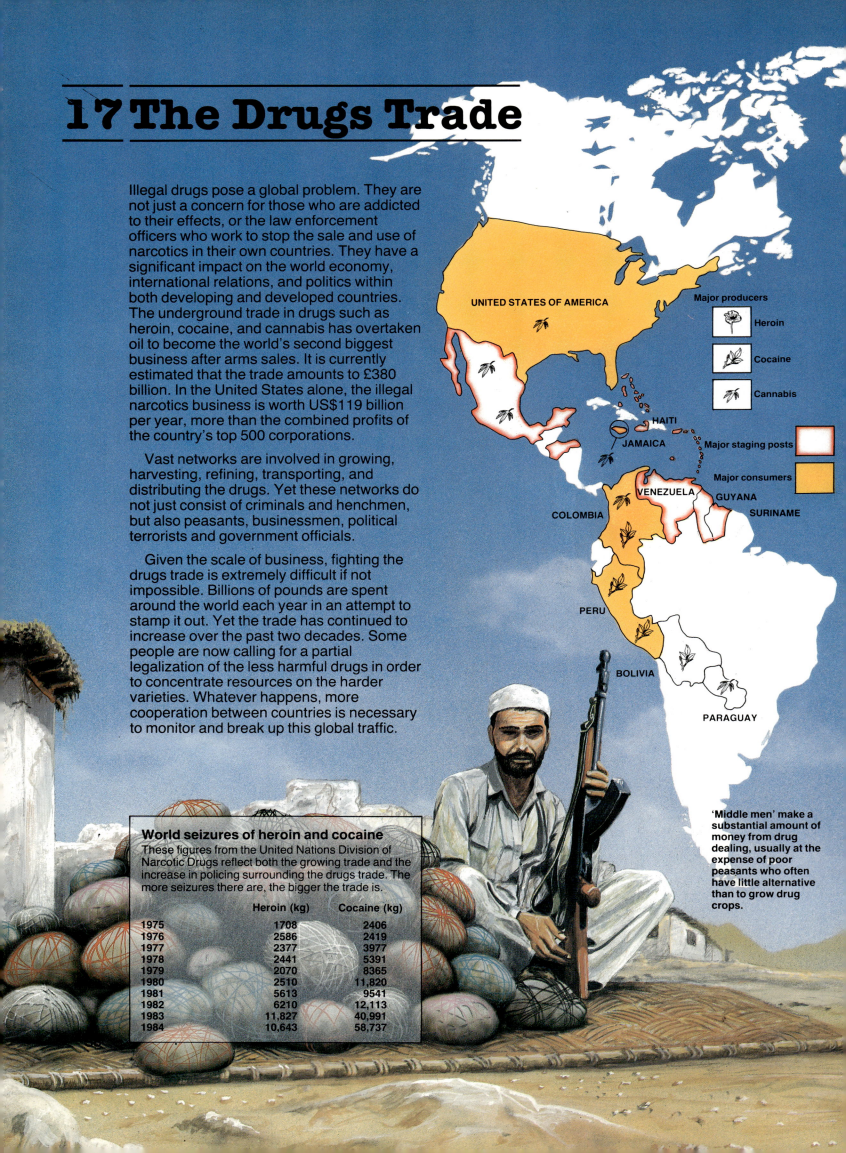

Major producers

- Heroin
- Cocaine
- Cannabis

Major staging posts

Major consumers

UNITED STATES OF AMERICA

HAITI
JAMAICA

VENEZUELA
GUYANA
COLOMBIA
SURINAME

PERU

BOLIVIA

PARAGUAY

'Middle men' make a substantial amount of money from drug dealing, usually at the expense of poor peasants who often have little alternative than to grow drug crops.

World seizures of heroin and cocaine

These figures from the United Nations Division of Narcotic Drugs reflect both the growing trade and the increase in policing surrounding the drugs trade. The more seizures there are, the bigger the trade is.

	Heroin (kg)	Cocaine (kg)
1975	1708	2406
1976	2586	2419
1977	2377	3977
1978	2441	5391
1979	2070	8365
1980	2510	11,820
1981	5613	9541
1982	6210	12,113
1983	11,827	40,991
1984	10,643	58,737

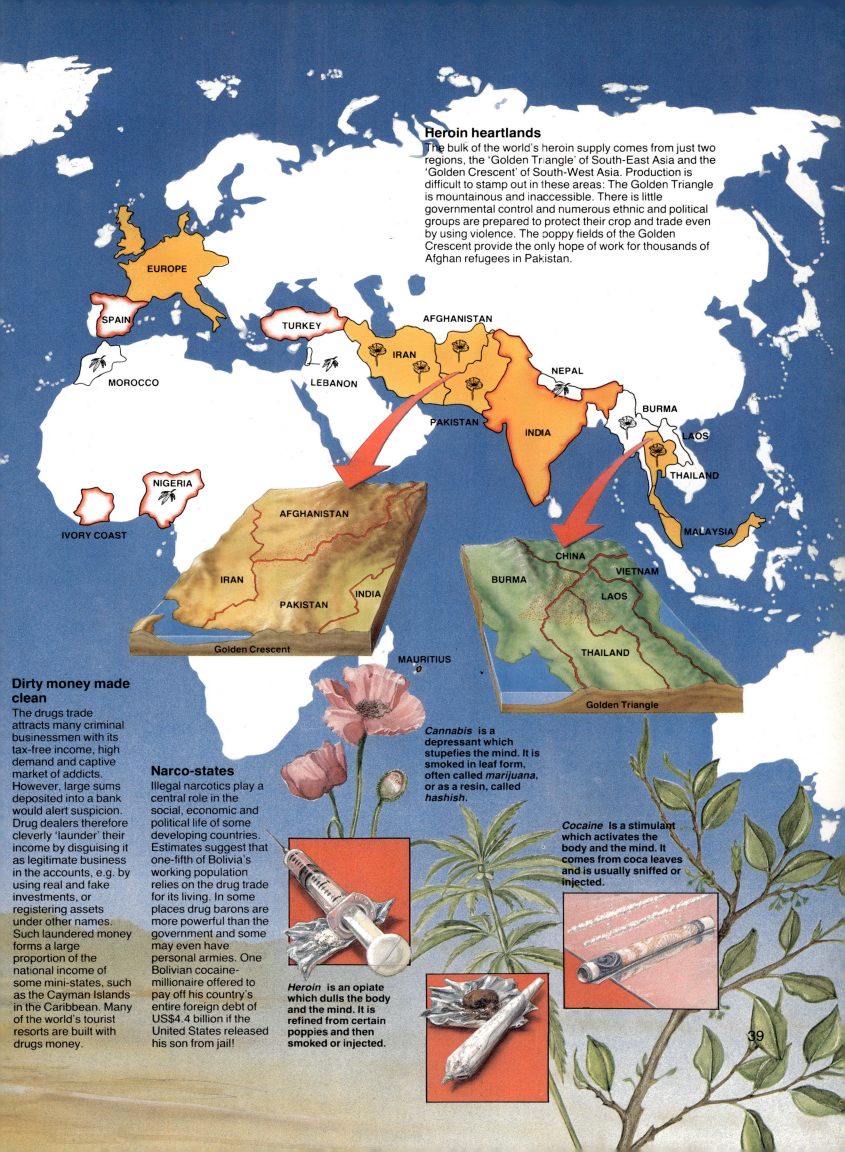

Heroin heartlands

The bulk of the world's heroin supply comes from just two regions, the 'Golden Triangle' of South-East Asia and the 'Golden Crescent' of South-West Asia. Production is difficult to stamp out in these areas: The Golden Triangle is mountainous and inaccessible. There is little governmental control and numerous ethnic and political groups are prepared to protect their crop and trade even by using violence. The poppy fields of the Golden Crescent provide the only hope of work for thousands of Afghan refugees in Pakistan.

EUROPE

SPAIN

TURKEY

AFGHANISTAN

MOROCCO

IRAN

LEBANON

NEPAL

BURMA

PAKISTAN

INDIA

LAOS

NIGERIA

THAILAND

IVORY COAST

AFGHANISTAN

MALAYSIA

IRAN

INDIA

CHINA

VIETNAM

PAKISTAN

BURMA

LAOS

Golden Crescent

THAILAND

MAURITIUS

Golden Triangle

Dirty money made clean

The drugs trade attracts many criminal businessmen with its tax-free income, high demand and captive market of addicts. However, large sums deposited into a bank would alert suspicion. Drug dealers therefore cleverly 'launder' their income by disguising it as legitimate business in the accounts, e.g. by using real and fake investments, or registering assets under other names. Such laundered money forms a large proportion of the national income of some mini-states, such as the Cayman Islands in the Caribbean. Many of the world's tourist resorts are built with drugs money.

Narco-states

Illegal narcotics play a central role in the social, economic and political life of some developing countries. Estimates suggest that one-fifth of Bolivia's working population relies on the drug trade for its living. In some places drug barons are more powerful than the government and some may even have personal armies. One Bolivian cocaine-millionaire offered to pay off his country's entire foreign debt of US$4.4 billion if the United States released his son from jail!

Cannabis is a depressant which stupefies the mind. It is smoked in leaf form, often called *marijuana*, or as a resin, called *hashish*.

Cocaine is a stimulant which activates the body and the mind. It comes from coca leaves and is usually sniffed or injected.

Heroin is an opiate which dulls the body and the mind. It is refined from certain poppies and then smoked or injected.

39

18 Malaria

Malaria is a debilitating disease caused by the *Plasmodium* parasite which is transmitted between humans by the *Anopheles* mosquito. Half the world's people live in areas where there is a risk of infection, and in 1980 there were 210 million chronic cases. Malaria causes headaches, fever and nausea and can lead to anaemia, kidney failure and

Pupa lavae in water

brain disease. Young children are at most risk and every year about 1 million Africans under 14 years old die. Those who survive are often sick periodically throughout their lives, as the parasite may stay in the body.

Malaria epidemics were common until the middle of the 20th century, causing a million fatalities a year in India alone. After World War II the World Health Organization directed a worldwide effort to eradicate malaria. In military-style campaigns, long-lasting insecticides such as DDT and dieldrin were sprayed on walls where the mosquitoes rested. However, this method proved very expensive, not always effective and the chemicals had harmful effects on the environment. Since the mid-1960s governments have adopted a more integrated approach with less ambitious targets. A wide variety of methods are used, including draining the pools in which the mosquitoes lay their eggs, spraying, drugs, repellants, and screens to protect houses. In many countries there has been complete success, but in others, particularly those too poor to afford all these methods, malaria persists.

A new problem has now arisen. The heavy use by the US army in Vietnam, of chloroquine, the safest and cheapest drug to treat malaria, enabled one deadly species of parasite to acquire immunity. It spread throughout the world, and no effective treatment has yet been found. Research now concentrates on finding a vaccine to innoculate entire populations.

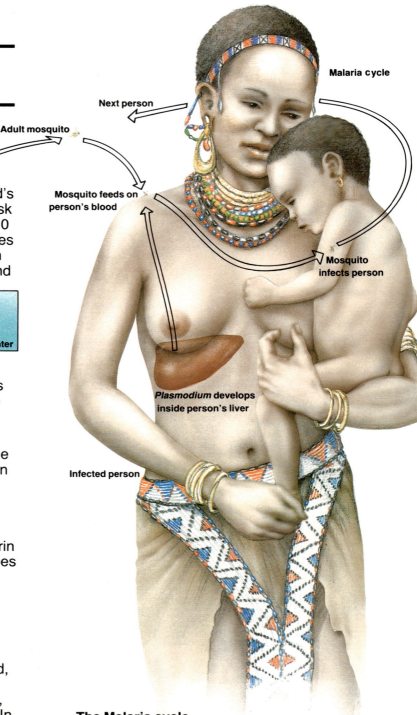

Malaria cycle

Next person

Adult mosquito

Mosquito feeds on person's blood

Mosquito infects person

Plasmodium develops inside person's liver

Infected person

The Malaria cycle

Malaria was recognized as far back as the fifth century BC, but it was not until the 1890s that the cycle connecting mosquitoes and parasites was identified. This enabled health workers to break the cycle in many countries. Since the mosquito could not fly far, it was possible to destroy its habitat of still water and create protective zones around settled areas.

The parasite

There are four species of *Plasmodium*, each with is own effects, reaction to drugs and geographical distribution:

P. Falciparum	the deadliest, resistant to chloroquine but unlike the others it does not stay long in the body
P. Vivax	being eliminated from the sub-tropics and temperate areas
P. Malaria	being eliminated from tropical areas
P. Orale	a mild form, confined to the forests of East and West Africa

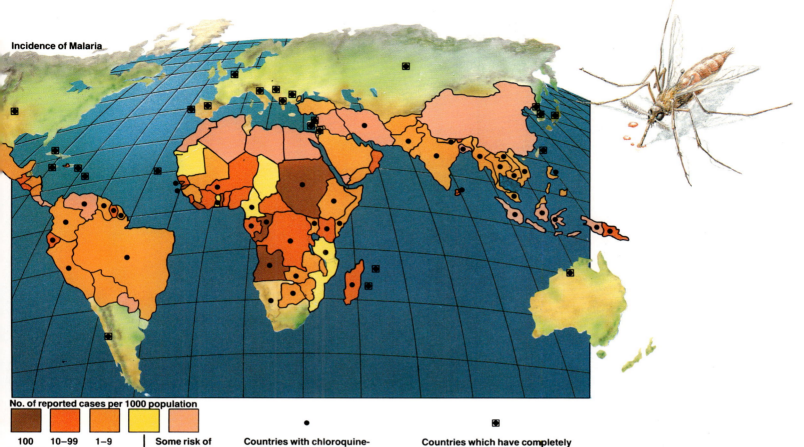

Incidence of Malaria

No. of reported cases per 1000 population

100 and over	10–99	1–9		Some risk of transmission

Known to have significant incidence but no figures reported

● Countries with chloroquine-resistant parasites

▣ Countries which have completely eradicated malaria since 1945

Incidence of malaria

The actual incidence of malaria is hard to establish, since many of the worst-affected countries lack comprehensive reporting methods. It appears that rates rose after 1965 and have fallen in the 1980s, but this may be because the number of countries providing records has fluctuated. Africa and Asia contribute 90% of all cases. A number of countries, such as Japan, Australia and the US have completely eradicated malaria since 1945.

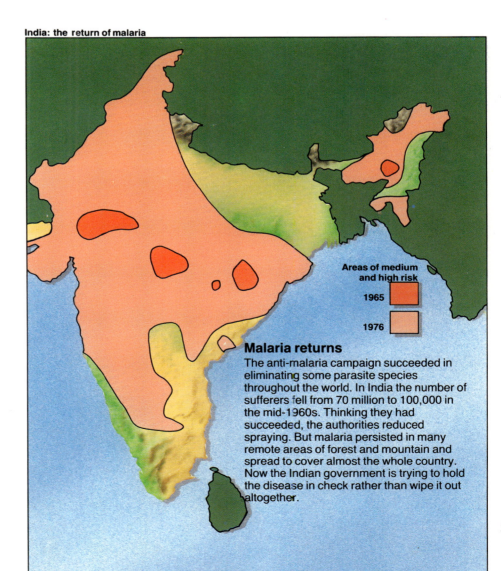

India: the return of malaria

Areas of medium and high risk

	1965
	1976

Malaria returns

The anti-malaria campaign succeeded in eliminating some parasite species throughout the world. In India the number of sufferers fell from 70 million to 100,000 in the mid-1960s. Thinking they had succeeded, the authorities reduced spraying. But malaria persisted in many remote areas of forest and mountain and spread to cover almost the whole country. Now the Indian government is trying to hold the disease in check rather than wipe it out altogether.

Malaria outside the tropics

Malaria was a common cause of sickness in lowland Europe for centuries. Since the 1600s the draining of marshes for farmland, the separation of dwellings from livestock buildings and improvements in nutrition have virtually wiped out the disease. Travellers still contract malaria, accounting for a few hundred cases per year.

France	23
West Germany	9
UK	8
Italy	6
Spain	6
US	5
Australia	1

19 AIDS

Acquired Immune Deficiency Syndrome (AIDS) was first diagnosed in 1981 and the virus which causes the disease, Human Immunodeficiency Virus (HIV), was identified two years later. At the end of 1988 133,000 cases of AIDS and 5 million HIV-infected persons were officially recognized world-wide. Despite not yet being one of the world's major killers, AIDS has become a matter of serious global concern.

One reason for this is the lack of knowledge about how the disease works or how it can be stopped. No one knows where it came from, though HIV is similar to some monkey viruses in Africa. It is known to be transmitted in bodily fluids such as blood and semen. Transmission can occur during sex, by sharing needles, in contaminated blood products, and between a pregnant woman and her foetus. High-risk groups therefore include sexually active individuals and drug addicts. In the West it spread first among homosexual men and users of blood products for medical treatment, but in Africa heterosexual sex and prenatal transmission appear to be more common causes of it spreading. HIV is difficult to detect and there is no foolproof test. It is not clear how many people infected with HIV will go on to get AIDS and how many will then die. HIV poses modern medical science one of its most challenging tasks.

Spreading the word
Many governments have undertaken large-scale publicity campaigns to warn people about AIDS and to encourage precautions, such as the use of rubber contraceptive sheaths, or condoms (pictured below). In Africa, Uganda led the continent by recognizing the disease and discouraging casual sex. Some countries such as Thailand were reluctant to publicize their problems for fear of harming the tourist trade. Although publicity does raise public awareness, the evidence that it alters the behaviour of high-risk individuals or groups is less clear.

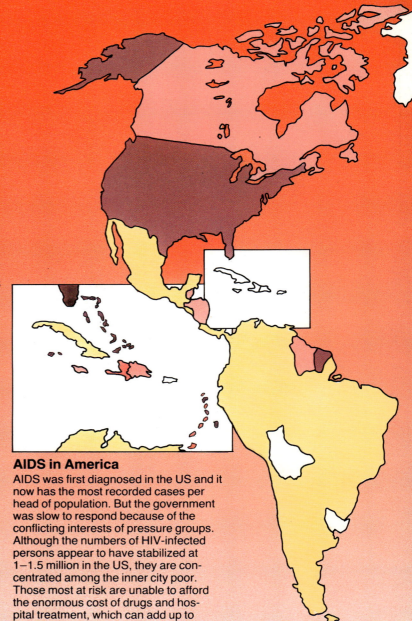

AIDS in America
AIDS was first diagnosed in the US and it now has the most recorded cases per head of population. But the government was slow to respond because of the conflicting interests of pressure groups. Although the numbers of HIV-infected persons appear to have stabilized at 1–1.5 million in the US, they are concentrated among the inner city poor. Those most at risk are unable to afford the enormous cost of drugs and hospital treatment, which can add up to $75,000 per year.

Blood Transfusion

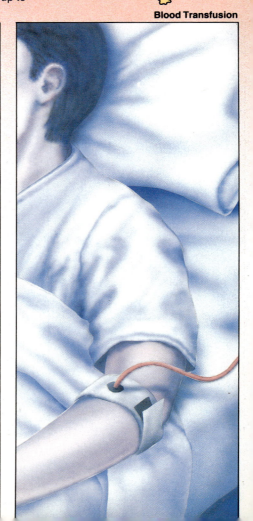

US AIDS victims by type of transmission, cumulative cases to September 1988

Adults	%
Homosexual/ bisexual male	63
Intravenous (iv) drug-user	19
Homosexual male and IV drug-user	8
Haemophilia/coagulation disorder	4
Transfusion blood/ coagulant	3
Undetermined	3
Total number of cases	71,609

Children	%
Parents with/at risk of AIDS	78
Transfusion blood/ components	13
Haemophilia/coagulation disorder	6
Undetermined	3
Total number of cases	1,157

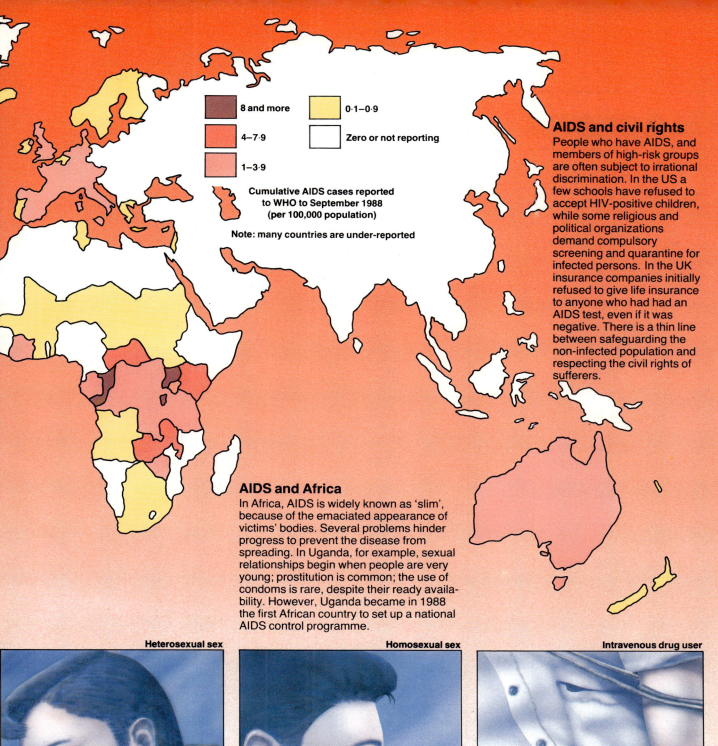

8 and more

4–7.9

1–3.9

0.1–0.9

Zero or not reporting

Cumulative AIDS cases reported
to WHO to September 1988
(per 100,000 population)

Note: many countries are under-reported

AIDS and civil rights

People who have AIDS, and
members of high-risk groups
are often subject to irrational
discrimination. In the US a
few schools have refused to
accept HIV-positive children,
while some religious and
political organizations
demand compulsory
screening and quarantine for
infected persons. In the UK
insurance companies initially
refused to give life insurance
to anyone who had had an
AIDS test, even if it was
negative. There is a thin line
between safeguarding the
non-infected population and
respecting the civil rights of
sufferers.

AIDS and Africa

In Africa, AIDS is widely known as 'slim',
because of the emaciated appearance of
victims' bodies. Several problems hinder
progress to prevent the disease from
spreading. In Uganda, for example, sexual
relationships begin when people are very
young; prostitution is common; the use of
condoms is rare, despite their ready availability. However, Uganda became in 1988
the first African country to set up a national
AIDS control programme.

Heterosexual sex

Homosexual sex

Intravenous drug user

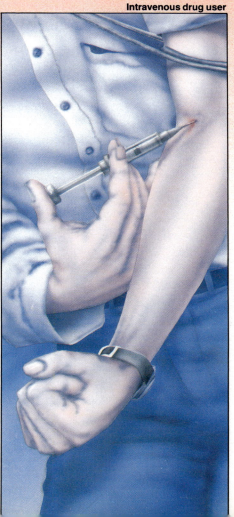

20 Racism

Racism is the belief that certain races (groups of people defined by physical characteristics) not only share common patterns of behaviour but that some are superior to others. Accompanying this belief is the idea that human civilization owes its progress to a given race, and that mixing races would mean its collapse.

Whereas throughout history cultural groups have often thought they were better than others, the idea that certain racial groups are superior has only come about during the last 300 to 400 years. In the art and literature of ancient, medieval and renaissance Europe, black and oriental figures were treated with the same respect and regard as the white Europeans. Yet since the great colonial expansions of the 15th century racist ideas have been increasingly popular. Racism is not a uniquely European phenomenon, but it has had its ugliest expression in Europe in the 20th century.

Racism can take many forms, from very subtle to harshly explicit. Prejudice and stereotyping affect attitudes and social interaction. Discrimination involves denying people homes, jobs, education and more. Segregation means keeping people separate in public places or neighbourhoods. Expulsion entails forcing people to leave an area or country. Genocide, or killing all members of a given physical type, is the most extreme expression of racism.

Right-wing parties with racist policies

 Size of vote at 1989 European elections (except in Norway)

Europe's new Right
Some European countries are witnessing increasing racism. It seems to be particularly directed against immigrant groups who have arrived since the late 1950s and 1960s (South Asians in England, North Africans in France, Turks in Germany). This racial violence has often been started by loosely organized neo-Nazi groups. Racist ideas and policies now play a large part in the manifestos of new right-wing political parties. In France the National Front gained over 14% of the vote in 1988, and in Germany the Republicans captured 7% in the 1989 European elections.

Banning racism
Societies wishing to prevent the violence associated with racism have two main options – either to create laws against discrimination or actively to help racial minorities gain jobs and university places. The 1964 Civil Rights Act, which followed years of struggle by black Americans, is regarded worldwide as a landmark for such laws. Many people argue that passing laws is not enough. They call for effective anti-racist policies.

America's Laws
1865 Slavery abolished
1896 Doctrine that races are 'separate but equal' upheld
1948 Armed forces desegregated
1954 Schools ordered to desegregate
1964–65 Civil Rights Acts, including Voting Rights Act to remove unfair political practices
1968 Housing discrimination outlawed

CRUSAD

Apartheid

Although racism is found in most societies, only in South Africa is all of social and political life organized around the principle of racial difference. Apartheid (or apart-ness) laws dictate where people can live and work, and under what conditions. Education, government, justice and freedom are all determined by race. Apartheid was devised and is supported by only the white minority. It gives no say to the three-quarters of the population who are black, and only limited powers to the smaller 'coloured' and Indian communities.

Apartheid policy depends both upon the clear definition by the state of which racial group a person belongs to, and upon geographical separation. All blacks are assigned to homelands, which the government claims are self-governing but which the world community refuses to recognize as such. The 11 million blacks who reside outside their homelands to work in mines, factories and towns, can only do so according to pass laws restricting their rights of movement.

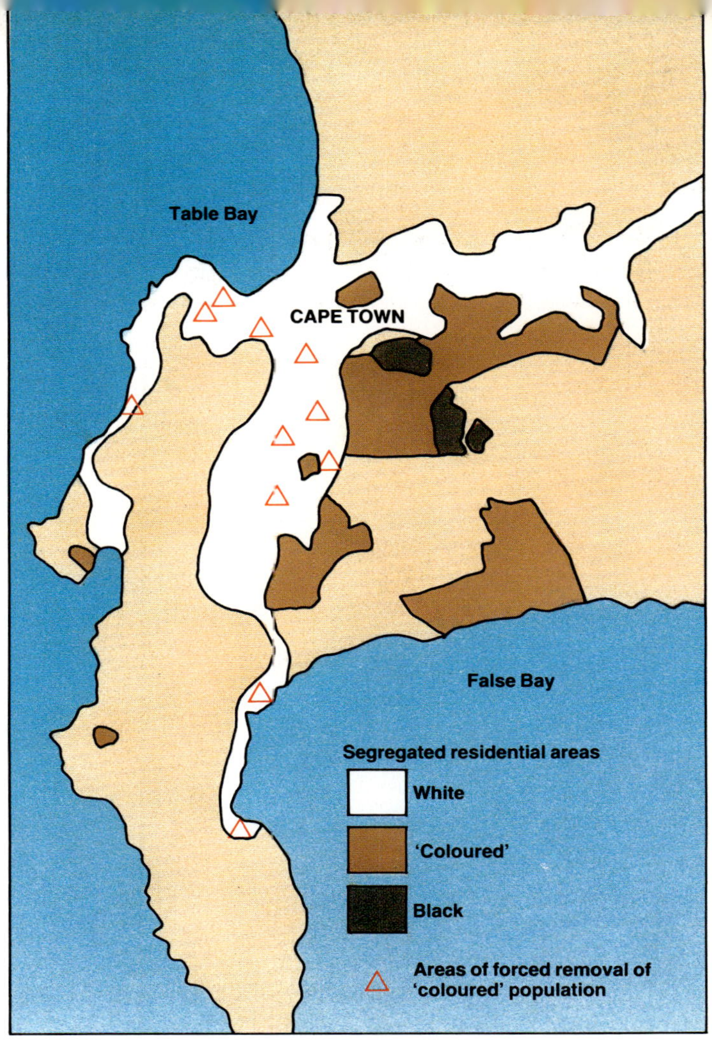

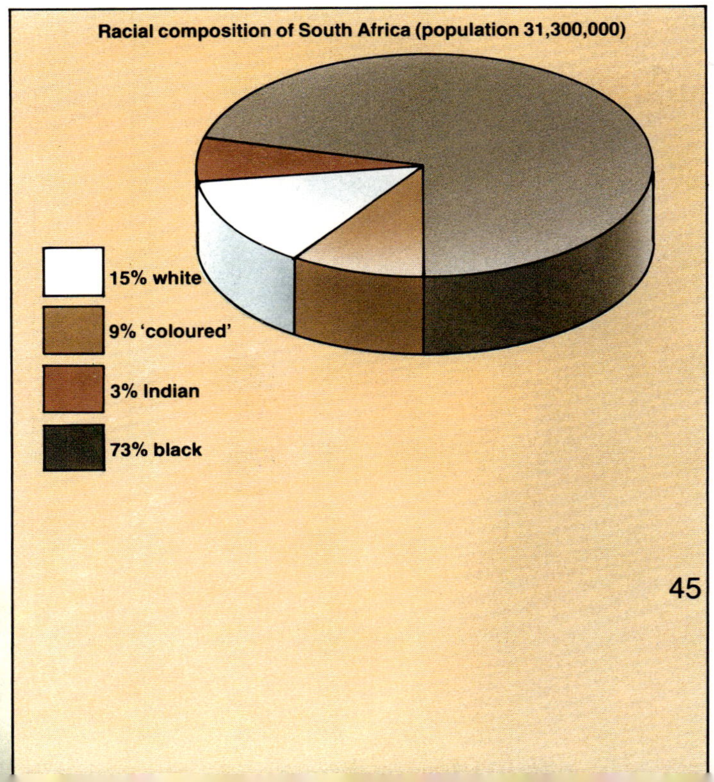

Power

ⓈORRUPTION

Table Bay

CAPE TOWN

False Bay

Segregated residential areas

- White
- 'Coloured'
- Black
- △ Areas of forced removal of 'coloured' population

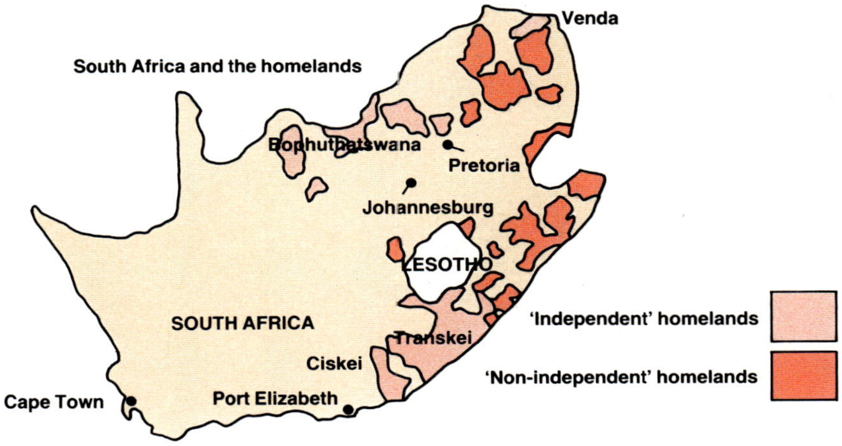

South Africa and the homelands

Venda

Bophuthatswana

Pretoria

Johannesburg

LESOTHO

SOUTH AFRICA

Transkei

Ciskei

Cape Town

Port Elizabeth

- 'Independent' homelands
- 'Non-independent' homelands

Racial composition of South Africa (population 31,300,000)

- 15% white
- 9% 'coloured'
- 3% Indian
- 73% black

45

21 Multiculturalism

In societies where a number of ethnic communities exist, policies have been developed which affect the rights and activities of these different groups. Sometimes governments which are largely comprised of members of one group, seek domination over all others by manipulating elections. They may also establish restrictions on the employment, economic activity, language, and cultural practices of members of other groups. In more democratic nations, 'multiculturalist' policies are advocated, whereby according to law, people of all communities are given equal economic, social, and political opportunities.

There are two basic types of multiculturalist policies. One type promotes cultural assimilation of minority groups: the values and customs of the majority are promoted as those which all citizens should publicly adopt, while minorities are encouraged to continue their cultural, religious and linguistic practices in private. The other type provides for cultural pluralism: that is, the customs, religious beliefs and languages of two or more communities are given equivalent status in institutions and representatives of the major ethnic groups have positions in government. Unfortunately, even legislation cannot guarantee equal treatment of minorities in daily life.

Peoples of the Soviet Union

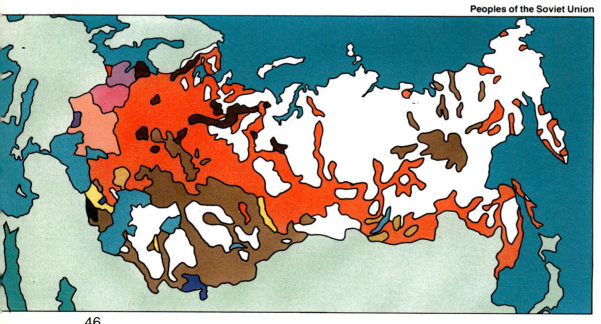

Soviet Union or Russian empire?

Just over half of the USSR's 260 million people are Russian. The census recognizes 93 nationality groups. In theory each group would have some self-government. In practice, because of migration and forced relocation, administrative boundaries did not always coincide with national ones.

Russians	Other Indo-Europe
Ukrainians	Finno-Ugrians
Belorussians	Turkics
Baltics	Mongolians
Romanians	Caucasians
Iranians	Sparsely populate

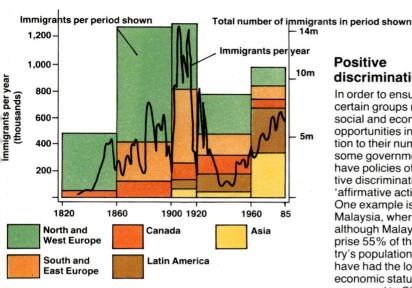

Legal immigration into the United States 1920–85

Immigrants per period shown — Total number of immigrants in period shown

- North and West Europe
- South and East Europe
- Canada
- Latin America
- Asia

The melting pot

The United States, like Australia and Canada, is essentially 'a land of immigrants' – a place where many different peoples have settled and adopted common traditions. Its basic policies, established in its constitution, are designed to have universal value to citizens of all ethnic backgrounds. Since the 19th century, the United States has received millions of people from almost everywhere in the world. However, the prominent sources of immigration have changed considerably over the past 150 years, bringing about a new ethnic makeup in many parts of the country. The result has been a move away from the country's European-dominated past.

Positive discrimination

In order to ensure that certain groups receive social and economic opportunities in proportion to their numbers, some governments have policies of 'positive discrimination' or 'affirmative action'. One example is Malaysia, where, although Malays comprise 55% of the country's population, they have had the lowest economic status when compared to Chinese and Indian residents. In response, the Government's *bumiputra* (princes of the soil) policy gives specific advantages to Malays in education, business, land ownership, and civil service jobs.

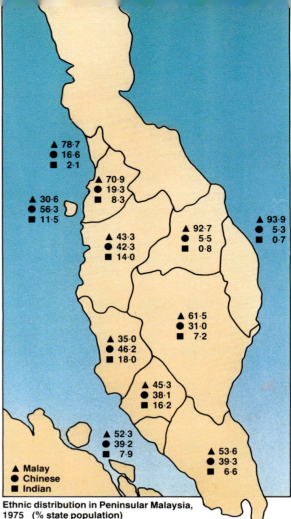

Ethnic distribution in Peninsular Malaysia, 1975 (% state population)

▲ Malay
● Chinese
■ Indian

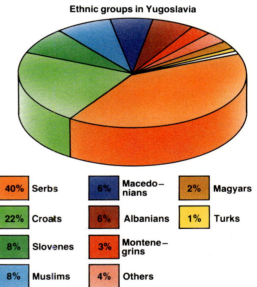

Ethnic groups in Yugoslavia

- 40% Serbs
- 22% Croats
- 8% Slovenes
- 8% Muslims
- 6% Macedonians
- 6% Albanians
- 3% Montenegrins
- 4% Others
- 2% Magyars
- 1% Turks

The federal solution

Yugoslavia has opted for a federal solution to the country's ethnic diversity. Each of six republics has its own powers, but since Serbs form the majority of the population, the other groups are concerned that they exercise too much power. In 1974 the Serbian republic granted a degree of independence to Kosovo, an Albanian-dominated area in the south. In recent years, however, Serbs outside Kosovo have joined with its small Serbian minority to demand that Serbia reestablish control over the courts, police, and defence. The problem with many federal systems is that state boundaries rarely coincide totally with the geographical distributions of ethnic groups.

Eradicating ethnicity

Bulgaria's policy toward its resident Turkish population of one million persons has been far from 'multiculturalist'. It has insisted that these people, who are spread throughout the country, are not really Turks but 'Bulgarian Muslims', remaining from when the region was part of the Ottoman empire. It has also insisted that the Turks change their names to Bulgarian ones. Bulgaria has prohibited the speaking of Turkish, and the reading and listening to Turkish newspapers and broadcasts. Those people who refused to drop their Turkish ethnicity and become 're-Bulgarized' began to leave the country as refugees. Ethnic riots and the liberalization of Bulgaria's ruling regime in 1989–90 may lead to a change in policy.

Main areas of Turkish population

47

22 Language

Language is much more than simply a means of communicating: it is a major social, economic, and political issue. There are only a few countries where all citizens speak the same native tongue, and in many there are hundreds of different languages used. Special legislation, and sometimes riots and civil wars have all arisen from the issue of language. Political strife and negotiations over language use have characterized nations as different as Canada, Burma, Belgium, Switzerland, Iran, and Sri Lanka.

Linguistic considerations are particularly important when countries promote an 'official' language: this is one which, according to law, is required in all schools, government offices, businesses, and public places. In many countries the official language is one inherited from a colonial past and may not even be spoken by the majority. In order to succeed socially and economically, immigrants and members of linguistic minorities must therefore adapt themselves to the language of the majority (or at least to that of those in power). Language use and rights thereby become prominent themes for most ethnic nationalist movements.

Bilingual education

A major issue confronting many countries is whether or to what extent education in immigrant languages should be provided. Those against bilingual education say everyone must be taught in the dominant language. Some people claim that bilingual education helps immigrant children make the transition to the dominant language. In the United States – where some 3.6 million students (80% of them Hispanic) are regarded as having poor English – the Supreme Court has ruled that education must be provided to all whether it is conducted in English or not. Ideally a pupil will speak two languages, although in some cities such as Los Angeles where over 100 tongues are taught in the schools such programmes place a considerable strain on educational resources.

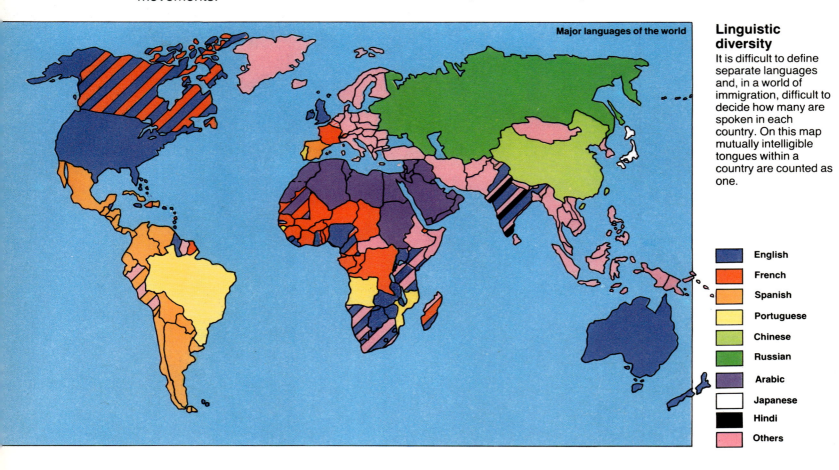

Major languages of the world

Linguistic diversity

It is difficult to define separate languages and, in a world of immigration, difficult to decide how many are spoken in each country. On this map mutually intelligible tongues within a country are counted as one.

- English
- French
- Spanish
- Portuguese
- Chinese
- Russian
- Arabic
- Japanese
- Hindi
- Others

Mixed languages

All languages are and always have been in a constant process of change. For instance, contemporary English is the process of several hundred years of accumulation from Anglo-Saxon, Latin, German, French, and Scandinavian languages. Since the great age of European colonial expansion dozens of newly mixed languages have been created. These are called either *pidgin* languages (where a few features from different languages are combined for specific communication, often in trade) or *creole* languages (mixed languages which have become more complex in order to be used by whole communities). Some mixed languages have even become national languages (such as in Papua New Guinea, Vanuatu, and Haiti).

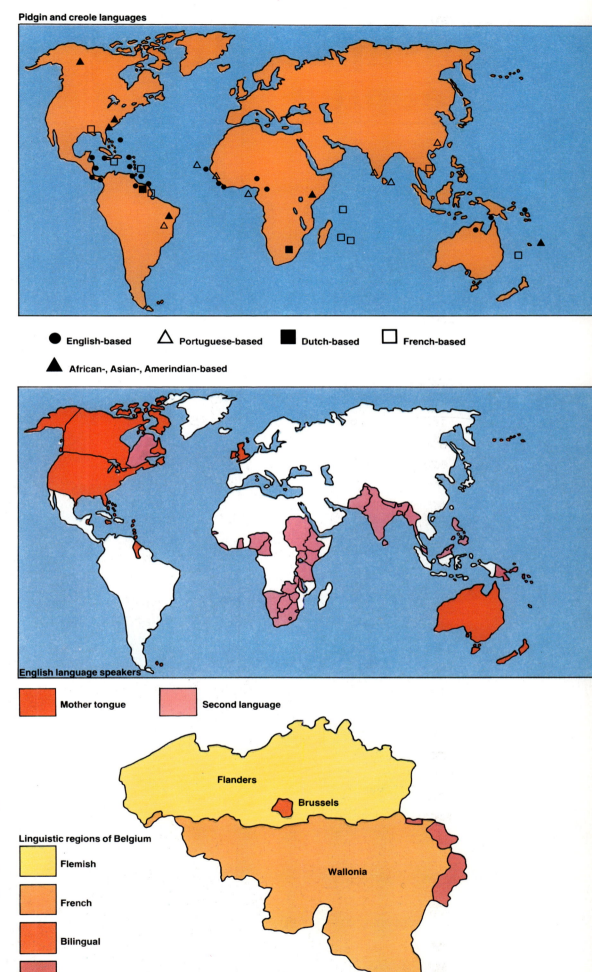

Pidgin and creole languages

● English-based   △ Portuguese-based   ■ Dutch-based   □ French-based

▲ African-, Asian-, Amerindian-based

An international language

Although the language with the greatest number of speakers, Mandarin Chinese, far exceeds all others, it is not very widespread in that it is almost only spoken in China. On the other hand English, the second largest language, is the official language of 60 countries around the world, although in many such countries it may not be widely spoken. Moreover, it has become the international business language, and three-quarters of all the world's mail is conducted in English.

English language speakers

■ Mother tongue   ■ Second language

A nation divided by language

When the state of Belgium was created in 1830 the French-speaking Walloons in the south of the country formed the dominant group. But within 100 years the demographic and economic balance shifted to the Flemish-speaking north and now the two communities are bitterly divided by the language issue. Political reforms introduced from 1970 onwards have created four linguistic and regional divisions within the country (the capital, Brussels, is officially bilingual), and forged a constitution which gives each community a fixed proportion of seats in the national legislative assembly. Flemish speakers make up 56% of the population, French speakers 32%, Germans 1% and 11% are counted as bilingual. Despite these reforms, the Walloons are pressing for even more regional autonomy.

Flanders

Brussels

Linguistic regions of Belgium

Wallonia

□ Flemish

□ French

□ Bilingual

□ German

23 Disappearing peoples

Aboriginal and 'indigenous' peoples are mainly found in the less industrialized parts of the world. For thousands of years they have lived close to their environment in small-scale societies (often called tribes), practising unique ways of life as nomadic herdsmen and hunters and gatherers. In some places, such as Mexico, they have been absorbed into the larger population through marriage, but in others, such as India, they remain distinct.

Contact with the West has brought much distress to indigenous peoples. Measles, smallpox and influenza struck down populations with no previous exposure to these diseases. In North America the native population fell from 12 to 3 million in three centuries of contact. War and slavery also took their toll. In the 20th century the processes of economic development, including mining, forestry and the creation of huge reservoirs and irrigation schemes, now threaten their lifestyles. Pacific Islanders have been removed from their lands for the testing of nuclear weapons, while thousands of nomads have been forced to settle permanently. Many indigenous peoples have no political rights. In some countries there are allegations of government attempts to exterminate entire indigenous peoples, known as 'ethnocide'. However, native peoples are now increasingly fighting back, claiming rights to the land and rights to continue their age-old ways of life.

▪ Limits of rainforest

Amerind nations

The Amerind (American Indian) population of South America numbers 19 million and is divided into over 450 separate and distinct nations, based on language, descent and territory. Over 90% live in the Andes, and the rest in lowland rainforests, where a small number practise wholly traditional lifestyles. Up to a quarter now live in cities, including several million in Lima, Peru. Ranching, gold, rubber, timber, tin and bauxite have attracted outsiders into the Amazon Basin. The Brazilian government is attempting to colonize the region by building roads and resettling the Indians in reservations, amid growing tension with the Yanomami Indians. Under Brazilian law, the Amerinds have no political rights and are regarded as wards of the state.

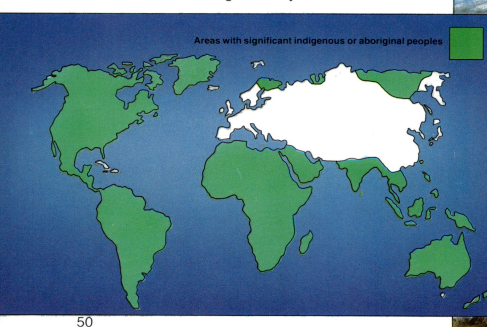

Areas with significant indigenous or aboriginal peoples ▪

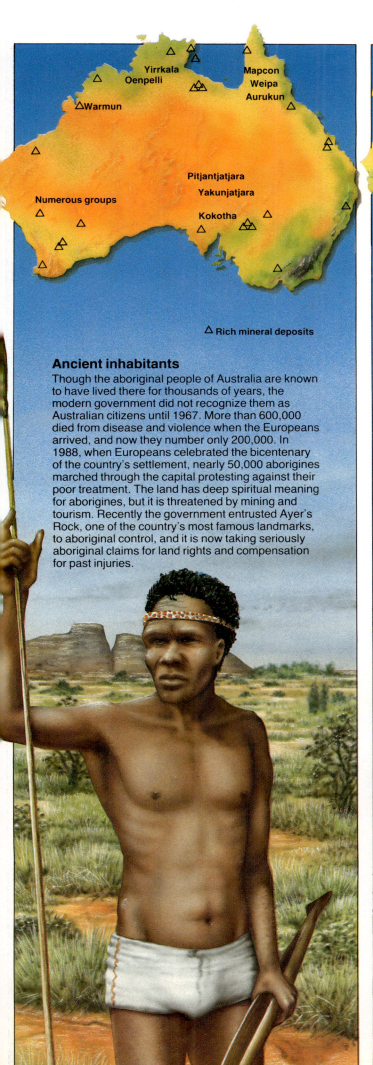

Yirrkala
Oenpelli
Mapcon
Weipa
Aurukun
Warmun
Pitjantjatjara
Yakunjatjara
Numerous groups
Kokotha

△ Rich mineral deposits

Ancient inhabitants

Though the aboriginal people of Australia are known to have lived there for thousands of years, the modern government did not recognize them as Australian citizens until 1967. More than 600,000 died from disease and violence when the Europeans arrived, and now they number only 200,000. In 1988, when Europeans celebrated the bicentenary of the country's settlement, nearly 50,000 aborigines marched through the capital protesting against their poor treatment. The land has deep spiritual meaning for aborigines, but it is threatened by mining and tourism. Recently the government entrusted Ayer's Rock, one of the country's most famous landmarks, to aboriginal control, and it is now taking seriously aboriginal claims for land rights and compensation for past injuries.

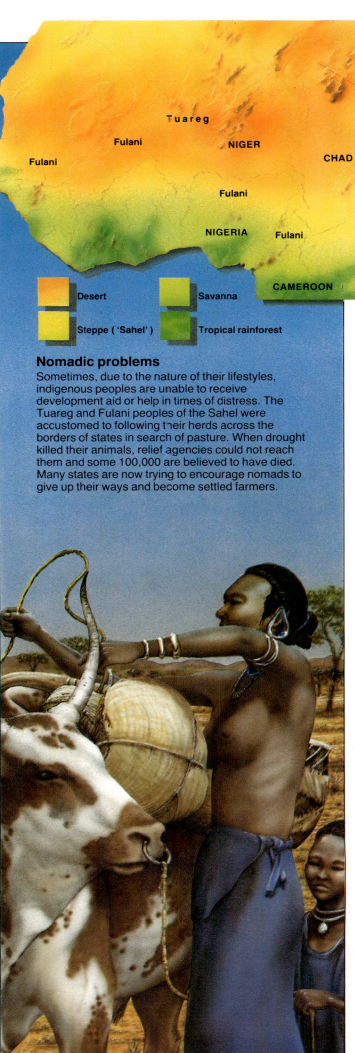

Tuareg
Fulani
NIGER
Fulani
CHAD
Fulani
NIGERIA
Fulani
CAMEROON

Desert
Savanna
Steppe ('Sahel')
Tropical rainforest

Nomadic problems

Sometimes, due to the nature of their lifestyles, indigenous peoples are unable to receive development aid or help in times of distress. The Tuareg and Fulani peoples of the Sahel were accustomed to following their herds across the borders of states in search of pasture. When drought killed their animals, relief agencies could not reach them and some 100,000 are believed to have died. Many states are now trying to encourage nomads to give up their ways and become settled farmers.

51

24 Personal Violence

We are living in an increasingly violent world. Violent crime rates are soaring (in the United States they rose by 270% between 1960 and 1980), and in many urban areas, people are afraid to leave their homes after dark or enter into 'no go' zones at any time. Yet even in the home violence is rife. More than half of all murders today arise from domestic disputes; wife battering and child abuse take place behind closed doors. One-third of all known rapes occur in the home (and very probably more, since it is estimated that 50–75% of rapes go unreported due to fears of further humiliation or police insensitivity). Stern prison sentencing and increased policing seem to be making little impact on this rising tide of violence.

What counts as 'violence' is often culturally relative: for instance, wife beating is accepted in some countries – and it has been only 25 years since this was made an offence in Britain. In Sweden, on the other hand, it is illegal for parents to hit their children.

There are a number of explanations for the increase in violence in cities. These include demographic factors (including the increase in the number of young people following the post was 'baby boom'), economic factors (suggesting that poverty and exploitation lead to violence), and social factors (such as overcrowding, inequality, or changing values).

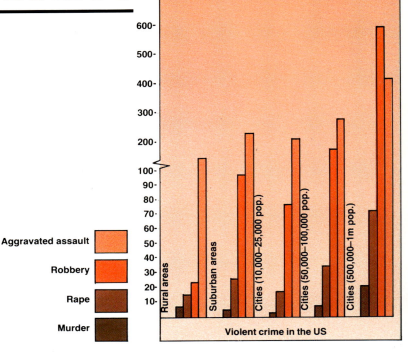

Violent crime in the US

Aggravated assault
Robbery
Rape
Murder

Incidence of violent crime in the US

Less than 1000 cases	50,000 – 100,000
1000 – 10,000	More than 100,000
10,000 – 50,000	

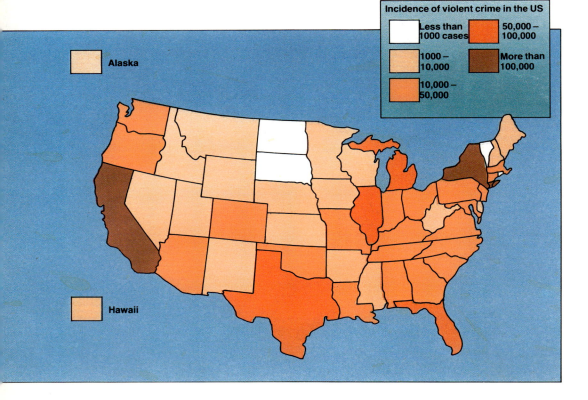

Alaska

Hawaii

Guns galore

Lax gun control laws in the United States have contributed to a huge number of murders and other forms of crime. In the United Kingdom – where guns are tightly controlled – there is approximately one gun for every 55 citizens; in the US there is one gun for every two citizens. In the early 1980s annual handgun deaths in the UK and Canada numbered 8, in Sweden 18, and in Switzerland 24. In the US they far surpassed 10,000.

TV violence

Many studies have been conducted regarding the relation between watching violence on television (from cartoons to police shows) and committing violence in real life).Though there is undoubtedly a rise in the frequency and explicitness of violence on TV and a marked rise in crime rates, researchers are still debating whether there is a causal link between the two. However, they do caution that overviewing televized violence may lead people to regard violence as acceptable.

Rank

1	
2	
3	
4	
5	
6	

'CRIME CLOCKS'
United States

Seconds

Minutes

Clocks show average frequency of crime; e.g. one assault every 5 seconds

Hooliganism

Since the mid 1960s, English football fans have gained an international reputation for violence. This reached a height following the incident at Heysel Stadium in Brussels in May, 1985, which resulted in 39 deaths. Yet violence among spectators has plagued the game in many places, including deaths at matches in Colombia, Sicily and Bangladesh. Researchers have suggested various causes for football related violence, from unemployment to changes in the game itself.

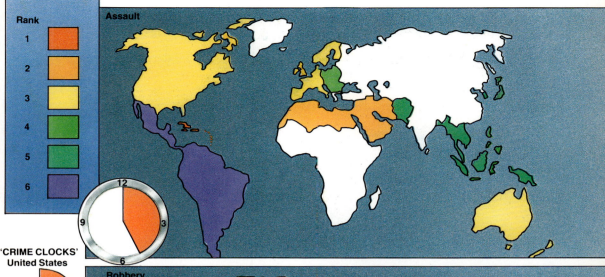

Assault

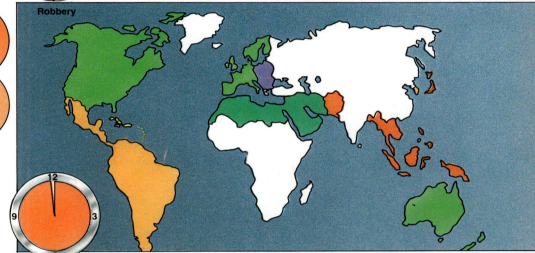

Robbery

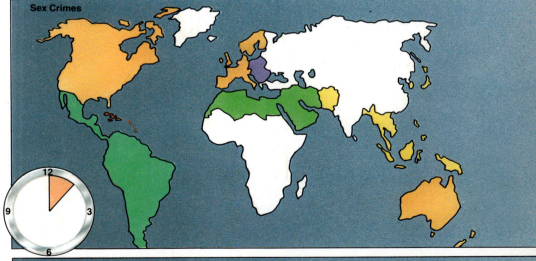

Sex Crimes

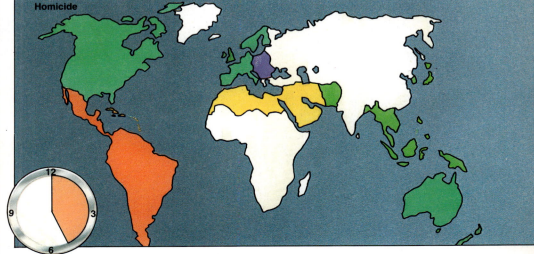

Homicide

53

25 Ethnic Separatism

Most countries of the world today contain a mixture of ethnic groups, communities which are conscious of a distinct history, language, religion and culture. Where such groups have become part of a state through conquest or by the imposition of political boundaries by colonial powers, they are often also geographically distinct. In many cases the concentration of ethnic identity in certain regions leads to separatism, the desire for separate political identity. The resulting movements demand a greater degree of political self-determination (the right to determine their future).

In some cases separatist movements want greater autonomy within an established state, which is known as regionalism. This might involve more say in decisions about education, language, taxes, local officials and the use of natural resources. Recently, for example, the Miskito Indians on the Caribbean coast of Nicaragua have achieved such ends. In other cases, the demand can be for separate statehood. This is known as secession. Such movements frequently involve civil war, as in Sudan or Ethiopia, terrorism, as in the Basque region of Spain, or popular uprisings as in the case of the Palestinians. Few states are willing to lose land without a fight. Sometimes secessionist movements are successful. Following a brief war in which nine million refugees were displaced, Bangladesh was created from Pakistan in 1971. More often the result is continued violence and repression.

Areas of strong regionalist sentiment in France

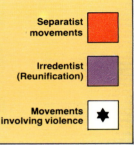

Separatist movements	(red)
Irredentist (Reunification)	(purple)
Movements involving violence	(star)

Ethnic resurgence in Europe

Modern European separatist movements have tended to be less violent and work through established political channels. Recently there has been a clear resurgence of ethnic or cultural feeling, especially in France, Spain and the United Kingdom, often as a reaction to increasing centralization of governmental power.

The French island of Corsica was developed by France after 1945, and many outsiders moved in, increasing the non-Corsican population from 10 to 45% over 30 years. Corsican separatists demanded more local control, using violence. The violence died down after the granting of elected assemblies to all regions of France. This gave Corsica control over economic development, agriculture, hydro-electric power, and transport.

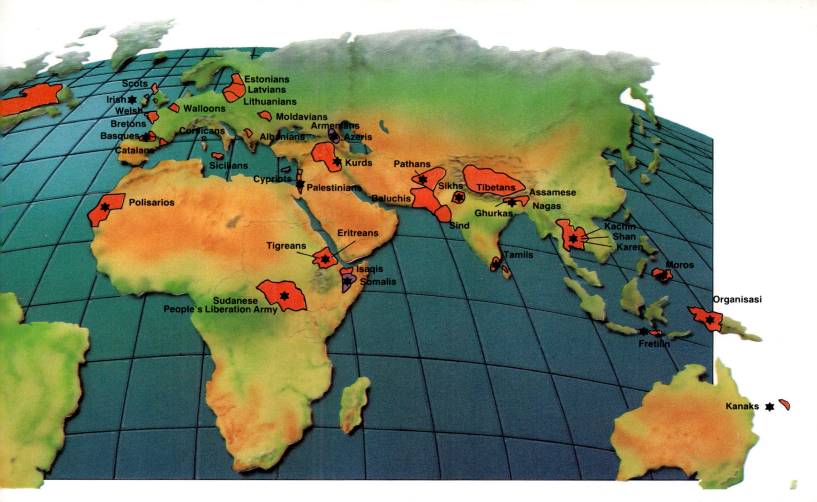

Scots · Irish · Welsh · Bretons · Basques · Catalans · Walloons · Corsicans · Sicilians · Cypriots · Palestinians · Estonians · Latvians · Lithuanians · Moldavians · Albanians · Armenians · Azeris · Kurds · Pathans · Baluchis · Sikhs · Sind · Ghurkas · Tibetans · Assamese · Nagas · Kachin · Shan · Karen · Moros · Tamils · Organisasi · Fretilin · Polisarios · Tigreans · Eritreans · Isaqis · Somalis · Sudanese People's Liberation Army · Kanaks

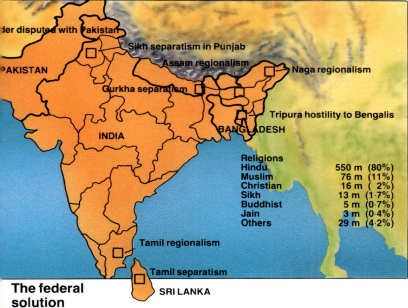

...der disputed with Pakistan · PAKISTAN · Sikh separatism in Punjab · Assam regionalism · Gurkha separatism · Naga regionalism · INDIA · BANGLADESH · Tripura hostility to Bengalis · Tamil regionalism · Tamil separatism · SRI LANKA

Religions		
Hindu	550 m	(80%)
Muslim	76 m	(11%)
Christian	16 m	(2%)
Sikh	13 m	(1·7%)
Buddhist	5 m	(0·7%)
Jain	3 m	(0·4%)
Others	29 m	(4·2%)

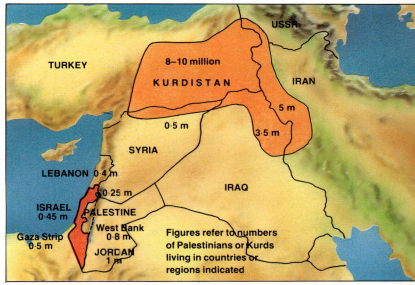

TURKEY · USSR · KURDISTAN 8–10 million · IRAN · 5 m · 0·5 m · 3·5 m · SYRIA · LEBANON 0·4 m · 0·25 m · ISRAEL 0·45 m · PALESTINE · West Bank 0·8 m · Gaza Strip 0·5 m · JORDAN 1 m · IRAQ · Figures refer to numbers of Palestinians or Kurds living in countries or regions indicated

The federal solution

One solution to separatism is that of a federal state, where the constitution allows for a division of powers and responsibilities between national and local levels. In certain matters, such as education, housing policy and taxation, the central state cannot intervene. Canada, India, Malaysia, and Nigeria are examples of federal states which enable ethnic groups to have some power.

India, with its vast area, huge population and ethnic diversity, could not easily be governed from a single centre. Despite its federal structure, however, there are still strong pressures for further fragmentation.

Sikh separatists, who form 60% of the population of Punjab, want the creation of a separate state, Khalistan. In 1984 Sikh extremists assassinated the Indian Prime Minister. There are also separatist movements in the east and south of India.

No homes in their homeland

Many ethnic groups have been left divided between states or dispersed and displaced by war. When the state of Israel was created in 1948, 4.7 million Palestinians were deprived of their homeland. They are now divided between Israel, areas occupied by Israel and adjacent countries. A similar fate has befallen the Kurds, 20 million of whom are divided between four countries. They are fighting for independence in Turkey, autonomy in Iran and federal status in Iraq.

26 Refugees

The 20th century has been called 'the century of refugees'. Though minority populations throughout history have been forced to migrate because of persecution in their homelands, the refugee phenomenon has reached dramatic proportions around the world in the last 70 years. The aftermath of destruction and the rise of new political régimes following both World Wars caused large sections of the population of Europe to become refugees (including Poles, Czechs, and Hungarians). In the 1960s and 1970s the area of greatest refugee displacement shifted dramatically from Europe to the Third World, where newly independent countries faced economic and political upheaval, natural disasters, and war. Today's global refugee population exceeds 12 million persons.

In the late 1970s the plight of Vietnamese 'boat people' turned the world's attention towards the dilemma of refugees. Yet problems of providing relief remain acute. Many countries which have received refugees, such as Pakistan and Sudan, are troubled by economic and social problems of their own. Refugees who fled across borders because of political struggles, for example in South Africa, Israel and Guatemala, have seen their camps attacked by armies. Starvation, disease, and psychological trauma also afflict refugees, and the relief agencies which assist them do so with minimal supplies and dwindling funds.

Major refugee movements to the US		
1956–57	Hungary	38,000
1960–65	E. Europe	20,000
1962–80	Cuba	836,000
1973–79	USSR (Jews)	36,000
1975–88	Indo-China	900,000

Europe

Haven for refugees

The United States is the world's major recipient of refugees. Since 1981 it has admitted over 650,000 people from all over the world. More than two-thirds have come from Indo-China and Cuba alone. The government places refugees in reception centres, where they obtain sponsorship from ordinary families willing to look after them. The original idea was to disperse the newcomers across the country as a way of encouraging them to adapt quickly to a new society. However, many subsequently migrated to be closer to their fellow nationals, creating large new refugee communities in cities like Los Angeles, New Orleans and Miami. Sometimes they have met with hostile reactions. In Louisiana and Texas Vietnamese fishermen were accused of encroaching upon the livelihood of American citizens.

Problem of definition

The 1951 United Nations Convention relating to the Status of Refugees defines a refugee as

'Any person who owing to well founded fear of being persecuted for reasons of race, religion, nationality, membership of a particular social group or political opinion, is outside the country of his nationality and is unable, or owing to such fear, is unwilling to avail himself of the protection of that country; or . . . is unwilling to return to it.'

This remains the official definition recognized by most countries in the world, but many experts believe it is increasingly obsolete. The definition leaves out, for instance, people who, because of drought, starvation, economic stagnation or political conflict, have lost their livelihood or found their living situation simply intolerable.

UNHCR

The United Nations High Commissioner for Refugees (UNHCR) was established to monitor the plight of refugees and assist in humanitarian attitudes worldwide. This body negotiates with governments over accepting, housing and providing political asylum for refugees. It serves as a channel for relief funding from numerous agencies to a variety of refugee programmes. Its total budget is US$371,576,000, which is largely designated towards caring for the everyday needs of refugees, mostly in Africa, Asia and the Middle East.

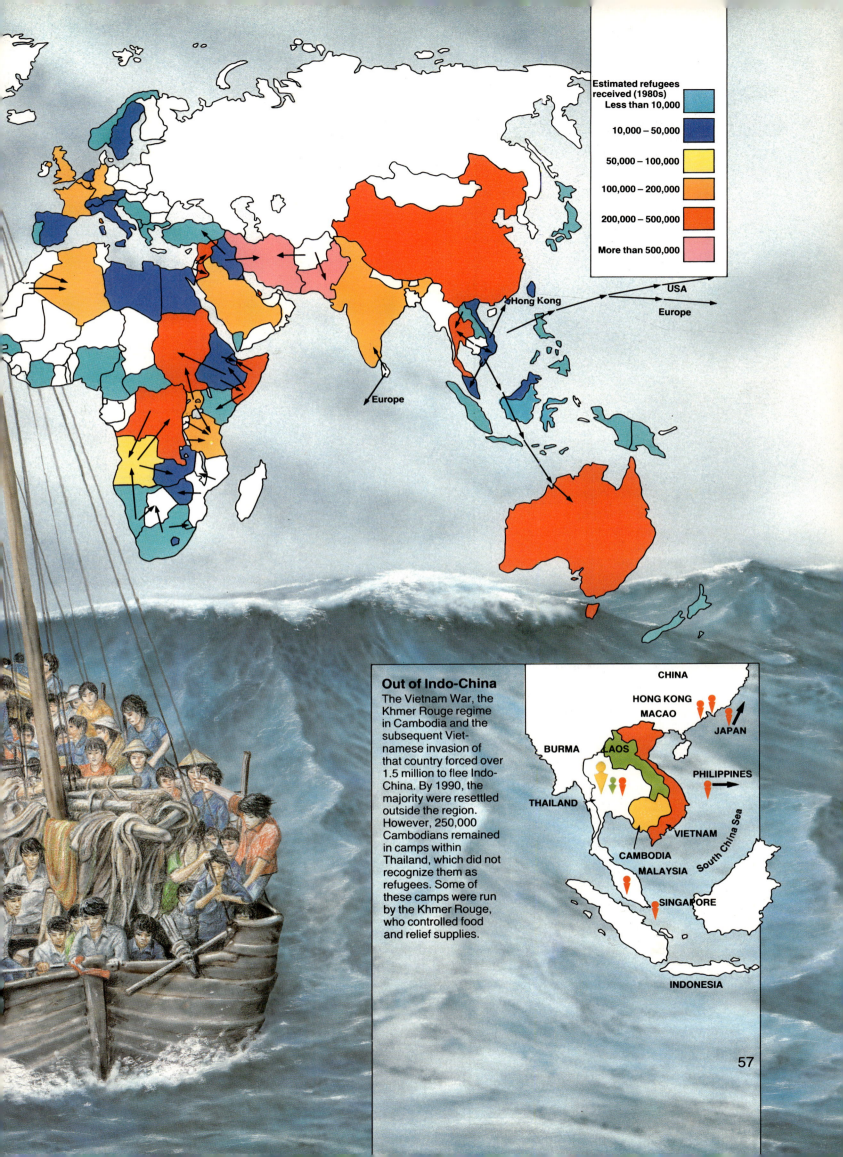

Estimated refugees received (1980s)

- Less than 10,000
- 10,000 – 50,000
- 50,000 – 100,000
- 100,000 – 200,000
- 200,000 – 500,000
- More than 500,000

USA

Europe

Hong Kong

Europe

Out of Indo-China

The Vietnam War, the Khmer Rouge regime in Cambodia and the subsequent Vietnamese invasion of that country forced over 1.5 million to flee Indo-China. By 1990, the majority were resettled outside the region. However, 250,000 Cambodians remained in camps within Thailand, which did not recognize them as refugees. Some of these camps were run by the Khmer Rouge, who controlled food and relief supplies.

CHINA

HONG KONG
MACAO

JAPAN

BURMA

LAOS

PHILIPPINES

THAILAND

VIETNAM

CAMBODIA

MALAYSIA

South China Sea

SINGAPORE

INDONESIA

57

27 Religion

As the world's population has increased in size and become more interlinked, the world's religions have likewise grown and come into increasing contact with each other. In the past people of different faiths came into contact through the expansion of empires and holy wars. From the 16th century, colonialism brought them together. For example, the British brought Hindus from India to colonies as far afield as East Africa, Fiji and the Caribbean as plantation workers or administrators. In more recent times world migrations have added to this diversity.

Many religions are truly global. Muslims live in over 160 countries, Hindus in 84, Buddhists in 84 and Jews in 112. Christianity is by far the world's largest faith. Its followers are spread over the globe in many separate denominations, and Christians form a majority in two-thirds of the world's countries.

Faith is sometimes seen as a private or personal matter, but it often gains public significance. Some states deny the right to practise religion. In others, people rally round religious symbols to advance their group interests. This can have violent consequences, such as in Lebanon (among Christians, Druzes, Muslims and their Jewish neighbours) and North India (among Hindus, Muslims and Sikhs).

Fundamentalism

In the past few decades there has been an upswing in the activities and numbers of fundamentalist groups within a number of religions. These hold a vehement, literal, and unswerving belief and application of the most basic scriptures and tenets of their tradition. They may be overtly hostile to members of other faiths. Examples include Christian fundamentalists in the US, estimated at 40 million in 1980. Through 1,400 radio stations and 65 nationwide TV programmes they are said to have helped bring about a conservative shift in American politics, publicizing such issues as compulsory prayers in schools and opposition to abortion. Perhaps most notably, Muslim fundamentalists overturned the ruler of Iran in 1979 and under their leader the Ayatollah Khomeini, inspired many Muslims around the world to follow their example.

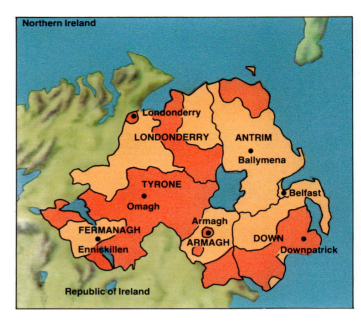

Protestant majority	Roman Catholic majority

When religion means more than religion

Faith is sometimes identified as the sole cause of conflict, but religious distinctions may be only one difference among many. For example, the community tensions and deep social divisions between Protestants and Catholics in Northern Ireland are not based on religion alone. The Protestants' numerical dominance in the North has allowed them to exercise political control but they fear that they would become a disadvantaged minority in a united Ireland.

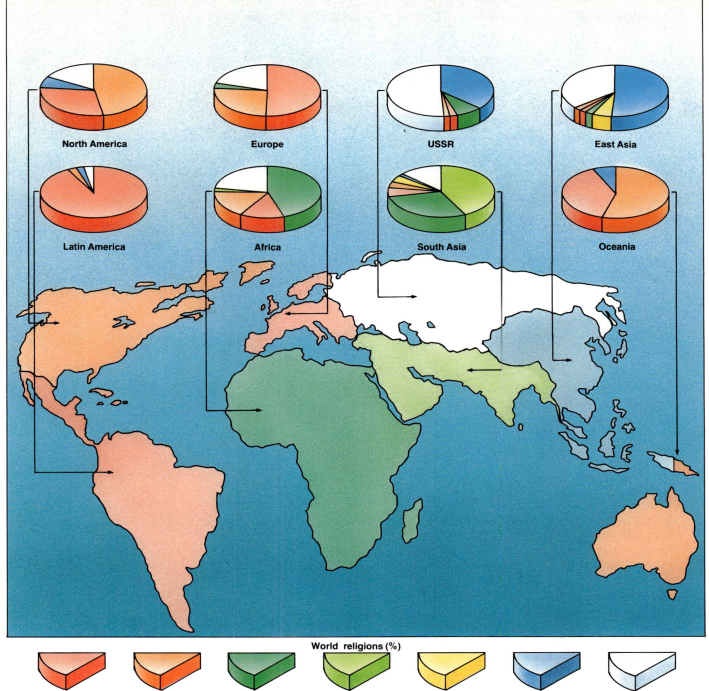

World religions (%)

| Roman Catholic | Protestant | Muslim | Hindu | Buddhist | Non-religious | Other |

Muslim majorities and minorities

Islam, though a relatively new religion begun in the 6th and 7th centuries AD, is now the second largest in the world. Its 817 million followers form 17% of the world's population, and live mostly in a continuous region stretching from Morocco to the Philippines. In a number of the 30 countries with Muslim majorities the laws and beliefs of Islam are part of the official state constitutions.

Muslims also form significant minorities. In the USSR, for example, they number 31.5 million and make up 11% of the population. They are concentrated in central Asia, and the fact that their birth rate is much higher than that of non-Muslims has caused tension. Soviet authorities are worried that Muslim unrest might spread into their country from Muslim countries in the south. There are signs of unrest in Tadzikhistan, and in Azerbaijan the Muslim majority is fighting the attempts of Christian Armenians to be reunited with the neighbouring state of Armenia.

Major Muslim populations in the Soviet Union

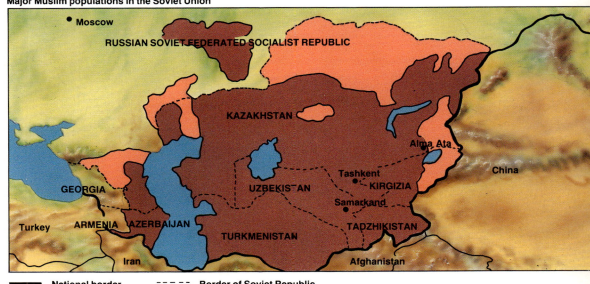

— National border   - - - - Border of Soviet Republic

50–85% Muslim   30–50% Muslim

28 Human Rights

The modern concept of human rights originated with such events as the French and American Revolutions, which produced the *Declaration des Droits de l'Homme et du Citoyen* (1789) and the Bill of Rights (1791). These documents include the right to the freedom of worship, the right to free speech, the right to vote in elections and equality before the law. These rights are commonly protected by the courts, which ideally should be free of government control or interference.

With the founding of the United Nations, a Universal Declaration of Human Rights was adopted by all participating countries in 1948. In the 1970s these became International Covenants which placed legal obligations to comply on the 77 signatory states.

Although human rights are now enshrined in many documents and declarations, many countries have not signed any agreements, and even those that have, occasionally break them. In one survey of 120 nations only 30 were found to honour the articles in the Universal Declaration. Only one in five of the world's people enjoy full human rights.

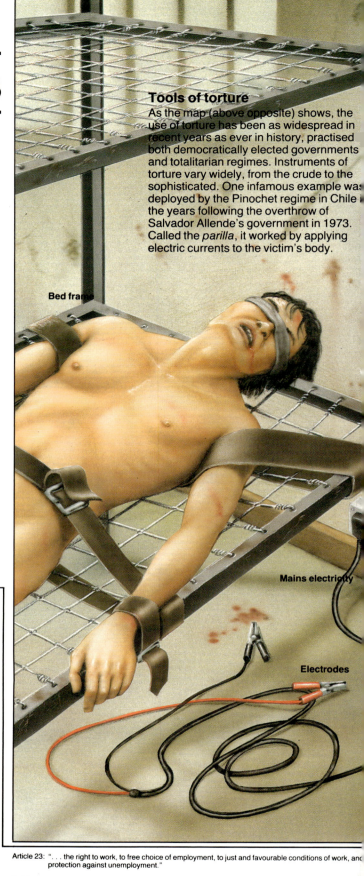

Tools of torture
As the map (above opposite) shows, the use of torture has been as widespread in recent years as ever in history, practised both democratically elected governments and totalitarian regimes. Instruments of torture vary widely, from the crude to the sophisticated. One infamous example was deployed by the Pinochet regime in Chile in the years following the overthrow of Salvador Allende's government in 1973. Called the *parilla*, it worked by applying electric currents to the victim's body.

Bed frame

Mains electricity

Electrodes

Universal Declaration of Human Rights

Article 1: "All human beings are born free and equal in dignity and rights . . ."

Article 2: "Everyone is entitled to all the rights and freedoms set forth in this Declaration, without distinction of any kind. . ."

Article 3: ". . . the right to life, liberty and the security of person."

Article 4: "No one shall be held in slavery or servitude. . ."

Article 5: "No one shall be subjected to torture or to cruel, inhuman, or degrading treatment or punishment."

Article 6: ". . . the right to recognition everywhere as a person before the law."

Article 7: "All are equal before the law and are entitled without any discrimination to equal protection of the law. . ."

Article 8: ". . . the right to an effective remedy by the competent tribunals for acts violating the fundamental rights granted him by the constitution or of the law."

Article 9: "No one shall be subjected to arbitrary arrest, detention or exile."

Article 10: "Everyone is entitled in full equality to a fair and public hearing by an independent and impartial tribunal. . ."

Article 11: ". . . Everyone charged with a penal offence has the right to be presumed innocent until proven guilty. . ."

Article 12: "No one shall be subjected to arbitrary interference with his privacy, family, home or correspondence, or to attacks upon his honour and reputation. . ."

Article 13: ". . . the right to freedom of movement and residence. . ."

Article 14: ". . . the right to seek and to enjoy in other countries asylum from persecution. . ."

Article 15: ". . . the right to a nationality. . ."

Article 16: ". . . the right to marry and found a family. . ."

Article 17: ". . . the right to own property alone as well in association with others. . ."

Article 18: ". . . the right to freedom of thought, conscience, and religion. . ."

Article 19: ". . . the right to freedom of opinion and expression. . ."

Article 20: ". . . the right to freedom of peaceful assembly. . ."

Article 21: ". . . the right to take part in the government of his country, directly or through chosen representatives. . ."

Article 22: ". . . the right to social security. . ."

Article 23: ". . . the right to work, to free choice of employment, to just and favourable conditions of work, and protection against unemployment."

Article 24: ". . . the right to rest and leisure, including reasonable limitation of working hours and periodic holi with pay."

Article 25: ". . . the right to a standard of living adequate for the health and well-being of himself and of his family. . ."

Article 26: ". . . the right to education. . ."

Article 27: ". . . the right freely to participate in the cultural life of the community. . ."

Article 28: "Everyone is entitled to a social and international order in which the rights and freedoms set forth Declaration can be fully realized."

Article 29: ". . . These rights and freedoms may in no case be exercised contrary to the purposes and princip the United Nations."

Article 30: "Nothing in this Declaration may be interpreted as implying . . . any right to engage in any activity aimed at the destruction of any rights and freedoms set forth herein."

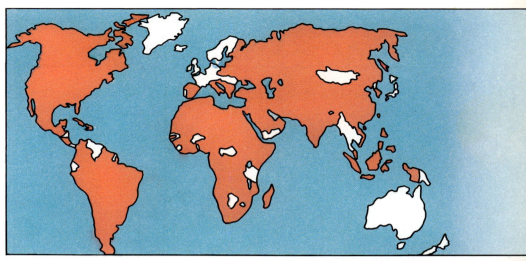

Torture in the eighties

Torture is one method of suppressing dissent. It may be used to gain information, destroy an individual's will or intimidate opponents. In their report 'Torture in the Eighties' Amnesty International investigated allegations and evidence of torture throughout the world between 1980 and 1983. Amnesty International exists to compare actual practice in a country with international principles of human rights, and then bring abuses to public attention and pressurize governments to change. It campaigns for the release of all prisoners of conscience, fair and prompt trials for political prisoners and the abolition of the death penalty.

Long history of military control | 10–20 years | More than 20 years

Repression

Based on the articles of a variety of international conventions on human rights, the nations of the world range from exemplary models of human freedom to the worst offenders against human dignity. Places like Sweden and the Netherlands come out on top, with extremely democratic government systems, complete independence of the media, free legal aid, and total commitment to monitoring human rights globally. On the bottom of such a world scale are countries such as Albania and the Central African Republic, where freedom of thought and expression are denied by means of torture and long detentions under harsh prison conditions. During the last forty years many Third World countries have at some time experienced repressive military governments. Because these governments force their way into power they must use force to maintain power, often waging fierce internal wars.

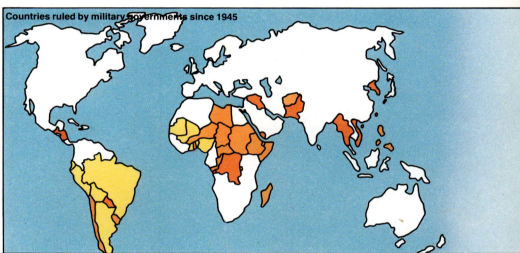

Countries ruled by military governments since 1945

International Covenant on Economic, Social and Cultural Rights

International Covenants on Civil and Political Rights

Both Covenants

Signatories of UN Covenants from 1976

The 'Disappeared'

Under the military regime in Argentina (1976–1983) between 7,000 and 10,000 individuals 'disappeared' – they were seized by the authorities and never heard of again. In 1977 a group called Abuelas de Plaza de Mayo ('Grandmothers of the Plaza de Mayo') began demonstrating every week to publicize the disappearance of 100 children. The regime has now been overthrown and many of its members are being tried. Some of the 'disappeared' have been traced after these trials. Identifying bodies in unmarked graves has become a major piece of forensic investigation. By 1986, 39 of the children had been found.

Glossary

Birth rate The number of live births per thousand population in a given year.

Counter-urbanization The movement of people and industries away from cities to rural areas, or from large cities to small towns.

Death rate The number of deaths per thousand population in a given year.

Developed and Developing countries No classification of countries into stages of development (see below) is entirely satisfactory. The World Bank classifies all countries with over one million inhabitants into (a) industrial market economies, members of the Organisation for Economic Cooperation and Development (19 countries); (b) high-income oil-exporters (4); (c) non-reporting countries, usually communist (9); (d) developing countries, split between low-income countries with a per capita income of less than $425 per year (39), and middle-income countries with a per capita income of more than $425 per year (58).

Development The process of growth in economic output, and the social, cultural and demographic changes which usually accompany it. Development is often measured by GNP (see below), but may also include measures of health, education and population change.

Ethnicity A collective identity held by a group of people often within a larger national population, that is based upon a combination of a common language, religion, history and customs.

Famine A scarcity of food which is accompanied by a breakdown in a country's economy, leading to widespread malnutrition, migration or death from starvation.

Federalism A constitutional arrangement in which political power and responsibility is clearly divided between a single central government and a number of regional or state governments.

Fertility The capacity of a population to reproduce itself through births.

GDP (Gross Domestic Product) The total worth of all goods and services produced within a country's economy by both residents and non-residents.

GNP (Gross National Product) The total worth of all goods and services produced by a country's resident population both at home and abroad.

Immigrant A person who arrives in another country with the intention of settling permanently.

Indigenous Belonging to a region or a country, often applied to people living in a part of the world before its conquest or settlement by outsiders.

Infant Mortality Rate In a given year, the number of infants per thousand live births who die before the age of one year.

Migrant An individual who moves to another country but who either intends to return home or is obliged by that country to return.

Nation A collective identity based upon self-government and a common territory which is either occupied by a group of people (e.g. the French) or is anticipated by a group (e.g. the Palestinians).

Nationalism Either the feeling of belonging to a nation, or the political attempt to form a sense of nationhood among a group of people. Nationalism may play an important part in struggles for independence or in conflict between or within countries.

Racism The belief (and practices based upon it) that different races of humankind each possess certain common and inherited physical and cultural characteristics, and that some races are naturally superior to others.

Refugee Defined by the United Nations as someone who, because of a well-founded fear of persecution based on either their race, religion, nationality, ethnicity or political views, cannot return to their country of origin without risking serious harm.

Religion A system of beliefs which usually involves the recognition of one or more supernatural entities, is justified by holy writings, and revolves around a set of distinct rituals.

Rural Relating to the countryside or non-urban places. Rural areas are usually defined in terms of low population density and a predominance of agriculture. Exact definitions vary between countries.

Separatism A belief in, and the movement for the creation of a separate political identity, often with complete independence. Separatism is usually supported by a geographically distinct group of people sharing common ethnicity (see above) within a state whose majority population exercises political power.

State Both a sovereign or self-governing territory and the institutions of government which possess the right to make and enforce laws, define citizenship, and enter into arrangements with other states (including war).

Urban Relating to towns or cities. Urban areas are usually defined in terms of large population size and high population density, although exact definitions vary between countries.

Urbanization The growth in the proportion of the population living in urban areas.

Index